GW01374330

departure
We support design

departure encourages individual creative and entrepreneurial performance

www.departure.at

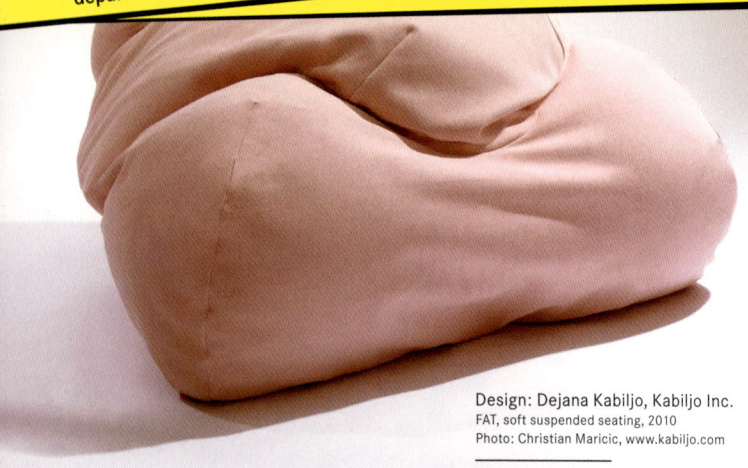

Design: Dejana Kabiljo, Kabiljo Inc.
FAT, soft suspended seating, 2010
Photo: Christian Maricic, www.kabiljo.com

departure is the City of Vienna's agency for the creative industries. Submission and information at www.departure.at

powered by: wirtschaftsagentur.at

AAD

VIENNA

edited by Isabella Klausnitzer

Art Architecture Design

teNeues

Intro ART	8	Seilerstätte Galleries	24	MuseumsQuartier	3
Augarten Contemporary	10	Thyssen-Bornemisza		Secession	4
KEX Kunsthalle Exnergasse	12	Art Contemporary	28	k/haus, Wien Museum Karlsplatz	4
BAWAG Contemporary	14	Portrait –		Belvedere	4
das weisse haus	16	Francesca von Habsburg	30	Schleifmühlgasse Galleries	5
COCO	18	Albertina	32	WestLicht	5
MAK	20	Eschenbachgasse Galleries	34	Essl Museum	5

Intro ARCHITECTURE	62	WAGNER:WERK		Gürtel	8
Die Bremer Stadtmusikanten	64	Museum Postsparkasse	74	Haus Ray1	9
Wohnbau Spittelau	66	Haas-Haus	78	Gasometer	9
Bahnhof Wien Praterstern	68	Looshaus	80	T-Center St. Marx	9
UNIQA Tower,		Architekturzentrum Wien	82	Wienerberg City	10
Sofitel Vienna Stephansdom	70	Portrait – Peter Noever	84	Kabelwerk	10

Intro DESIGN	108	Portrait – Bernd Schlacher	126	Song / Song Song	14
Hollmann Beletage	110	First Floor	128	Unger und Klein	14
The Ring –		Restaurant Design by		Blumenkraft, Mood	15
Vienna's Casual Luxury Hotel	112	Hermann Czech	130	Lichterloh	15
Das Triest	116	Loosbar	134	Park	15
Skopik & Lohn	120	DO & CO World	136		
Motto World	122	Naschmarkt	140		

Map	156	Service	160	Credits // Imprint	16

ART
ARCHITECTURE
DESIGN
VIENNA

AAD Content

INTR

Isabella Klausnitzer

"What should I see?" is the usual question I get from international friends when they come to visit Vienna. What they really want to know are what sorts of things they should visit that are not listed in the usual guidebooks. It was not always easy for contemporary art, architecture and design to stand out against the incomparable scenery and the impressive history of the city. However, with the active support of the city, the "new Vienna" has been able to successfully draw attention to itself on the international scene, and new hot spots continue to pop up. I have asked people in creative circles in Vienna, "What do you show your friends when they come to town?" This book presents these personal recommendations—sometimes subjective, emotional, and often surprising. Vienna has many such insider tips to offer because the arts scene has grown immensely in recent years. No matter how many times you've visited Vienna, each one of these places will form the beginning of a journey that will lead you to make new and exciting discoveries.

„Was soll ich mir anschauen?", ist die regelmäßige Frage meiner internationalen Freunde, wenn sie nach Wien kommen. Sie meinen damit jene Dinge, die normalerweise nicht in den klassischen Reiseführern zu finden sind. Für zeitgenössische Kunst, Architektur und Design war es nicht immer leicht, sich gegen die unvergleichliche historische Kulisse und die beeindruckende Geschichte der Stadt durchzusetzen. Das „neue Wien" hat sich aber, mit aktiver Unterstützung der Stadt, in den letzten Jahren international stark bemerkbar machen können. Neue Hotspots sind entstanden bzw. gerade im Entstehen. Ich habe Kreative unserer Stadt gefragt: „Was zeigt Ihr Euren Freunden, wenn sie nach Wien kommen?" Genau diese persönlichen Empfehlungen präsentiert dieses Buch. Teilweise subjektiv, emotionell und oft überraschend. Wien hat viele dieser Geheimtipps, denn die Szene ist in den letzten Jahren ungemein gewachsen. Und jeder der Orte ist für sich wieder der Beginn einer Reise, auf der auch die, die schon oft in unserer Stadt waren, neue, aufregende Entdeckungen machen werden.

« Que dois-je voir? ». Voici la question que me posent mes amis étrangers quand ils viennent à Vienne. Ils sous-entendent par là toutes les curiosités que l'on ne trouve pas dans les guides touristiques classiques. En matière d'art contemporain, d'architecture et de design, il n'est pas toujours facile de s'imposer aux incomparables décors historiques ni à l'impressionnante histoire de la capitale. En collaboration avec la ville de Vienne, le concept du « Nouveau Vienne » s'est ostensiblement distingué au niveau international ces dernières années. De nouveaux lieux incontournables ont été créés ou sont en cours de réalisation. J'ai demandé à des artistes viennois : « Que montrez-vous à vos amis quand ils viennent à Vienne ? ». C'est exactement ce genre de conseils personnels que vous trouverez dans cet ouvrage. Parfois subjectifs, émotionnels mais souvent surprenants. Vienne est truffée d'endroits « coup de cœur », car ce milieu s'est considérablement développé ces dernières années. Et chaque lieu est aussi pour ceux qui connaissent déjà la ville le début d'un nouveau voyage.

"Che cosa mi consigli di vedere?": è la tipica domanda che amici di altre nazionalità mi pongono quando arrivano a Vienna. Intendono dire quelle cose che in genere non si trovano nelle guide turistiche comuni. Per quanto riguarda arte, architettura e design contemporanei, non era sempre facile spuntarla sull'incomparabile panorama storico e lo stupefacente passato di questa città. Negli ultimi anni, però, la "nuova Vienna" è riuscita a farsi notare considerevolmente sul piano internazionale, grazie anche al concreto sostegno offerto dalla città. Sono così sorti, o stanno nascendo, nuovi luoghi di grande interesse. Ho chiesto alle persone più creative della nostra città: "Cosa mostrate ai vostri amici quando vengono a Vienna?". Il presente libro contiene proprio questi consigli personali. A volte soggettivi, a volte impulsivi e spesso sorprendenti. A Vienna sono molti i luoghi di questo tipo che ancora pochi conoscono, poiché negli ultimi anni il panorama cittadino si è evoluto in modo straordinario. E ciascuno di questi posti è di per sé l'inizio di un nuovo viaggio, durante il quale anche quanti sono già stati più volte nella capitale austriaca saranno protagonisti di nuove, entusiasmanti scoperte.

ART

A

Vienna has not been content to rest on the laurels of its Baroque and Jugendstil heritage; instead, it has pushed forward to become a center for contemporary art as well. Large public institutions such as the Secession, the MuseumsQuartier, Albertina, or MAK reflect this attitude as do the vibrant scenes revolving around galleries and private exhibitions. The various gallery districts—and we introduce the most important ones—each offer a wide range of contemporary works, all within walking distance. Many well-known artists with an international reputation such as Erwin Wurm, Hubert Scheibl or Eva Schlegel live and work in this city. Aside from displaying art, Vienna continues to cultivate the personal contact between art aficionados and artists at many different art events and nurtures discourse about art. Private patrons, such as Francesca Thyssen-Habsburg, the Essl family or companies such as BAWAG or Generali, set a strong course in the arts scene with their collections and exhibitions.

Wien ruht sich nicht auf seinem künstlerischen Erbe aus dem Barock und Jugendstil aus, sondern ist auch Zentrum zeitgenössischer Kunst. Die großen öffentlichen Institutionen wie Secession, MuseumsQuartier, Albertina oder MAK spiegeln dies genauso wider wie die äußerst lebendige Galerien- und private Ausstellungsszene. Die verschiedenen Galerienviertel, von denen wir die wichtigsten vorstellen, bieten jeweils in Gehdistanz eine breite Palette zeitgenössischer Werke. Viele namhafte Künstler mit internationalem Format wie Erwin Wurm, Hubert Scheibl oder Eva Schlegel leben und arbeiten in dieser Stadt, die neben der Präsentation der Werke immer wieder in vielen Kunstevents den persönlichen Kontakt zwischen Kunstinteressierten und Künstlern und einen Kunstdiskurs fördert. Private Mäzene wie Francesca Thyssen-Habsburg, die Familie Essl oder Firmen wie BAWAG oder Generali setzen mit ihren Sammlungen und Ausstellungen ebenfalls starke Akzente in diesem Bereich.

INTRO ART 9

Vienne n'est pas seulement la ville du baroque et de l'Art nouveau, elle est aussi celle de l'art contemporain. Les grandes institutions publiques comme Secession, MuseumsQuartier, Albertina ou MAK, tout comme les différentes galeries et expositions privées en sont la preuve. Les différents quartiers de galeries, dont les plus importants sont ici présentés, proposent chacun un vaste éventail d'œuvres d'art contemporain. De nombreux artistes mondialement célèbres comme Erwin Wurm, Hubert Scheibl ou Eva Schlegel vivent et travaillent à Vienne. Des artistes qui, hormis le fait d'exposer leurs chefs d'œuvre, favorisent le contact avec les passionnés d'art et cultivent un discours artistique lors de différents événements. Avec leurs collections et expositions, des mécènes privés tels que Francesca Thyssen-Habsburg, la famille Essl ou des entreprises comme BAWAG ou Generali donnent également une forte impulsion au domaine artistique.

Vienna non solo vanta un ricco patrimonio artistico risalente al periodo del Barocco e dello Jugendstil, ma è anche un centro dell'arte contemporanea. Lo dimostrano le grandi istituzioni pubbliche quali il Palazzo della Secessione, il MuseumsQuartier, l'Albertina e il MAK, come pure il panorama estremamente vivace offerto da gallerie e mostre d'arte private. I vari quartieri dei musei, dei quali vi presentiamo i più importanti, offrono un'ampia gamma di opere d'arte contemporanea facilmente raggiungibili a piedi l'una dall'altra. Molti rinomati artisti di fama internazionale, come Erwin Wurm, Hubert Scheibl o Eva Schlegel, vivono e lavorano in questa città, che oltre a presentare le opere, nell'ambito di numerosi eventi di carattere artistico cerca spesso di incentivare il contatto diretto tra appassionati d'arte e artisti e un relativo confronto di idee. Dal canto loro, mecenati privati come Francesca Thyssen-Habsburg, la famiglia Essl e società quali BAWAG o Generali propongono collezioni e mostre private che stimolano ulteriormente il panorama artistico cittadino.

AUGARTEN CONTEMPORARY

Scherzergasse 1a // 2nd district, Leopoldstadt
Tel.: +43 (0)1 795 57-0
www.belvedere.at

Thu–Sun 11 am to 7 pm
Tram 2, 5 Am Tabor

ART 11

In the Augarten, the oldest Baroque garden complex in Vienna, the Belvedere runs the Augarten Contemporary. Redesigned by Vienna architect Susanne Zottl, this hall has been used for special exhibitions of contemporary art—paintings, drawings, photography, video, installations—since 2001. Since its renovation, the Augarten Contemporary also housed an artist's apartment with a studio for artists in residence. Another section of the building complex includes a museum dedicated to Austrian sculptor Gustinus Ambrosi.

Im Augarten, der ältesten barocken Gartenanlage Wiens, betreibt das Belvedere die Dependance Augarten Contemporary. Seit 2001 finden in der von der Wiener Architektin Susanne Zottl neu gestalteten Halle Ausstellungen zu zeitgenössischer Kunst – Malerei, Zeichnung, Fotografie, Video, Installation – statt. Ferner gibt es seit dem Umbau eine Künstlerwohnung mit Atelier für Artists in Residence. Ein Teil des Gebäudekomplexes beherbergt ein dem österreichischen Bildhauer Gustinus Ambrosi gewidmetes Museum.

Dans l'Augarten, le plus ancien jardin baroque de Vienne, le Belvédère exploite l'Augarten Contemporary. Depuis 2001, dans la salle d'exposition restructurée par l'architecte viennoise Susanne Zottl, des expositions d'art contemporain (peinture, dessin, photographie, vidéo, installation) sont proposées. De plus, une maison d'artistes avec atelier a été créée pour les artistes. Une partie du complexe abrite également un musée dédiés au sculpteur autrichien Gustinus Ambrosi.

Presso l'Augarten, il giardino barocco più antico di Vienna, il Belvedere gestisce la Augarten Contemporary. Dal 2001, nel padiglione ristrutturato dall'architetto viennese Susanne Zottl sono allestite mostre di opere d'arte contemporanea che spaziano dalla pittura alle installazioni, passando per il disegno, la fotografia e i video. Il complesso comprende anche un appartamento per artisti con atelier denominato "Artists in Residence". Un'ala dell'edificio ospita un museo dedicati allo scultore austriaco Gustinus Ambrosi.

A

KEX KUNSTHALLE EXNERGASSE

Währinger Straße 59, access via staircase 2, 1st floor //
9th district, Alsergrund
Tel.: +43 (0)1 401 21-41 or -42
kunsthalleexnergasse.wuk.at

Tue–Fri 1 pm to 6 pm, Sat 11 am to 2 pm
U6 Währinger Straße/Volksoper

ART 13

Hidden in an idyllic courtyard visitors will find the entrance to Kunsthalle Exnergasse on the second floor of the WUK Cultural Center, a former locomotive factory. The open approach of offering space for exhibitions and projects of innovative, experimental and contemporary art has found its architectural equivalent in the bright 4.300-sq.-ft. exhibition hall, where interdisciplinary events such as symposiums, lectures, readings, or concerts are held as well.

Etwas versteckt im idyllischen Hof liegt der Eingang zur Kunsthalle Exnergasse in der ersten Etage des Kulturzentrums WUK, einer ehemaligen Lokomotivenfabrik. Der offene Ansatz, Raum für Ausstellungen und Projekte innovativer, experimenteller und zeitgenössischer Kunst zu bieten, findet seine architektonische Entsprechung in der 400 m² großen, lichtdurchfluteten Ausstellungshalle, in der auch interdisziplinäre Veranstaltungen wie Symposien, Vorträge, Lesungen oder Konzerte stattfinden.

La Kunsthalle Exnergasse, dont l'entrée légèrement dérobée se trouve dans une sublime cour, se situe au premier étage du centre culturel WUK, une ancienne usine de locomotives. Cet espace de 400 m², inondé de lumière et arborant une architecture intéressante, offre un espace d'exposition et de production dédié à l'innovation et l'expérimentation dans l'art contemporain. Des symposiums, conférences, lectures ou concerts y sont par ailleurs organisés.

L'entrata alla Kunsthalle Exnergasse, ospitata al primo piano del centro culturale WUK (una ex fabbrica di locomotive), si trova un po' nascosta nell'incantevole cortile del palazzo. Il dichiarato obiettivo di offrire spazio a mostre e progetti di arte innovativa, sperimentale e contemporanea trova realizzazione in una luminosissima sala espositiva di 400 m² in cui si tengono anche manifestazioni interdisciplinari come simposi, conferenze, letture e concerti.

A

BAWAG CONTEMPORARY

Franz-Josefs-Kai 3 // 1st district, Innere Stadt
Tel.: +43 (0)599 059 19
www.bawagcontemporary.com

Daily 2 pm to 8 pm
U1, U4 Schwedenplatz, Tram 1 Julius-Raab-Platz

ART 15

In May 2010, BAWAG Contemporary moved to its new location in a former tile showroom on Franz-Josefs-Kai where it will continue to showcase contemporary art. The gallery provides a forum for young artists to exhibit their work to a wider audience, often for the very first time. Concerts, video screenings and performances round out the program. On the street facade of the gallery, architects propeller z used bar-code-like black enameled glass panels to make a striking statement on the building's exterior.

Seit Mai 2010 zeigt die BAWAG Contemporary in einem ehemaligen Kachelschauraum am Franz-Josefs-Kai Gegenwartskunst. Die vorgestellten jungen Künstler präsentieren ihre Arbeit hier oft zum ersten Mal einem breiteren Publikum. Konzerte, Videoscreenings und Performances vervollständigen das Programm. An der Straßenfassade des Kunstraums wurde von den Architekten propeller z mit strichcodeartigen, schwarz emaillierten Glasfeldern auch nach außen hin ein markantes Zeichen gesetzt.

Dans la Franz-Josef-Kai, le BAWAG Contemporary expose depuis mai 2010 de l'art contemporain dans une pièce ayant autrefois servi à exposer des carreaux. De jeunes artistes y présentent leur travail à un large public et ce, souvent pour la première fois. Des concerts, visionnages de vidéos et performances complètent le programme. Avec la façade côté rue de la salle le ton est donné d'emblée. Les architectes propeller z l'ont animée de surfaces noires émaillées rappelant des codes barre.

Da maggio 2010 il BAWAG Contemporary presenta mostre di arte contemporanea nella cornice di una ex show-room di piastrelle di Franz-Josefs-Kai dove spesso giovani artisti si presentano per la prima volta davanti a un grande pubblico. Concerti, proiezioni di video e spettacoli di vario genere completano il programma. La struttura si fa notare anche all'esterno per la sua facciata concepita dallo studio di architettura propeller z, la quale arricchisce la strada con una serie di alte finestre in vetro nero smaltato che ricordano un codice a barre.

A

The somber architecture of this former government building on Wollzeile Street forms a striking contrast to the young contemporary paintings, object and concept art on display on the fourth floor of das weisse haus—at least until the general renovation of the building has been completed. The fifth floor houses "work in progress" project spaces for young artists for three months at a time. On the ground floor, the porter's lodges provide space for changing installations.

Die nüchterne Architektur des ehemaligen Amtsgebäudes in der Wollzeile bildet einen reizvollen Kontrast zur jungen zeitgenössischen Malerei, Objekt- und Konzeptkunst, die der Kunstverein das weisse haus – bis zur Generalsanierung des Gebäudes – im vierten Stockwerk präsentiert. Auf der fünften Etage stehen jungen Kunstschaffenden Projekträume für jeweils drei Monate „work in progress" zur Verfügung. Zusätzlich werden die Portierslogen im Erdgeschoss mit wechselnden Installationen bespielt.

L'architecture sobre de l'ancien bâtiment administratif situé dans la Wollzeile contraste fabuleusement avec la peinture contemporaine et l'art conceptuel contemporain qui y sont présentés au quatrième étage, jusqu'à la rénovation complète du bâtiment, par l'association artistique das weisse haus. Au cinquième étage, des espaces sont mis à disposition de jeunes artistes durant trois mois dans le cadre d'un programme « work in progress ». Les loges de concierge situées au rez-de-chaussée sont mises en scène à l'aide d'installations temporaires.

Lo spoglio stile dell'edificio in Wollzeile, un tempo adibito a funzione amministrativa, crea un interessante contrasto con la pittura contemporanea e le opere d'arte oggettuale e concettuale che l'associazione das weisse haus presenta – fino all'inizio dell'intervento di risanamento generale dell'edificio – al quarto piano del palazzo. Grazie al progetto "work in progress", al quinto piano sono a disposizione per tre mesi degli spazi per giovani artisti. Le aree di ingresso sono invece adibite all'allestimento di installazioni temporanee.

ART 17

DAS WEISSE HAUS

Wollzeile 1, 4th + 5th floor // 1st district, Innere Stadt
Tel.: +43 (0)664 840 49 12
www.dasweissehaus.at

Tue–Fri 3 pm to 8 pm, Sat noon to 5 pm
U1, U3 Stephansplatz

COCO (short for "Contemporary Concerns") uses a subtitle—Exhibitions, Theory, Bar—that concisely describes what this art association is all about. Located in a passage on the Bauernmarkt in Vienna's inner city, curator Severin Dünser and artist Christian Kobald run this space for contemporary art and show paintings, objects, installations, videos, and performances in the two exhibition spaces. COCO also hosts mini-symposiums, film screenings and lectures; afterwards visitors can continue their discussions over cocktails at the bar.

Kurz und prägnant macht der Untertitel „Ausstellungen, Theorie, Bar" deutlich, worum es dem Kunstverein COCO (kurz für Contemporary Concerns) geht. In einer Passage am Bauernmarkt betreiben Kurator Severin Dünser und Künstler Christian Kobald ihren Raum für zeitgenössische Kunst und zeigen in zwei Ausstellungsräumen Malerei, Objekte, Installationen, Videos und Performances. Minisymposien, Filmscreenings und Vorträge begleiten das Programm, und anschließend kann an der Bar bei Cocktails weiterdiskutiert werden.

« Expositions, théorie, bar », voici le résumé parfait du concept de l'association artistique COCO (Contemporary Concerns). Dans un passage de la Bauernmarkt, Severin Dünser, le directeur, et Christian Kobald, artiste, gèrent un espace dédié à l'art contemporain où ils présentent des tableaux, objets, installations, vidéos et performances dans deux salles d'exposition. Des mini-symposiums, des visionnages de films ainsi que des conférences complètent le programme et les discussions peuvent se poursuivre au bar, autour d'un cocktail.

Sintetico e conciso, "Esposizioni, teoria, bar" spiega chiaramente qual è l'essenza dell'associazione artistica COCO (Contemporary Concerns). Gestita dal curatore Severin Dünser e l'artista Christian Kobald, l'associazione si occupa di arte contemporanea e trova spazio presso il Bauernmarkt, dove sono allestite due sale che ospitano mostre di pittura, oggetti artistici, installazioni, video e spettacoli. Il programma è corredato da piccoli simposi, proiezioni di film e seminari, al termine dei quali si può continuare a discutere davanti a un cocktail al bar.

ART 19

COCO

Bauernmarkt 9 // 1st district, Innere Stadt
Tel.: +43 (0)699 116 58 112
www.co-co.at

Thu–Sat 4 pm to 8 pm (gallery)
Fri 8 pm to 2 am (bar)
U1, U3 Stephansplatz

A

MAK

Headed by Peter Noever since 1986, MAK has housed large single-artist exhibitions by Franz West, Elke Krystufek, Peter Eisenman, or Anish Kapoor. By creating innovative exhibitions from the permanent collection and putting on top-class symposiums, MAK has positioned itself as a central interface for contemporary art, design, and architecture. Special projects are held at the MAK Depot of Contemporary Art in the Arenbergpark flak tower, which is slated to house the Contemporary Art Tower (CAT) project for the 21st century collection.

Seit 1986 hat sich das MAK unter Führung von Peter Noever mit großen Einzelschauen zu Franz West, Elke Krystufek, Peter Eisenman oder Anish Kapoor, innovativ inszenierten Ausstellungen aus der ständigen Sammlung und hochkarätig besetzten Symposien als zentrale Schnittstelle für Gegenwartskunst, Design und Architektur positioniert. Sonderprojekte laufen im MAK-Gegenwartskunstdepot Gefechtsturm Arenbergpark, für den im Rahmen des Projekts CAT – Contemporary Art Tower die Sammlung des 21. Jahrhunderts in Planung ist.

ART | 21

Depuis 1986, le MAK, dirigé par Peter Noever, se situe à la jonction de l'art contemporain, du design et de l'architecture. Des expositions individuelles de Franz West, Elke Krystufek, Peter Eisenman ou Anish Kapoor sont présentées et les œuvres de la collection permanente sont mises en scène de manière innovante. Dans la tour de l'Arenbergpark, le Dépôt d'art contemporain du MAK, organise des symposiums et mène des projets exceptionnels. Dans le cadre du projet CAT, il accueillera la collection du XXIe siècle, actuellement en planification.

Dal 1986 il MAK, sotto la direzione di Peter Noever, si è imposto come grande interfaccia tra arte contemporanea, design e architettura, offrendo importanti vetrine a singoli artisti come Franz West, Elke Krystufek, Peter Eisenman o Anish Kapoor, innovativi metodi espositivi delle collezioni permanenti e simposi d'alta levatura. Sono in corso progetti speciali nel Deposito di Arte Contemporanea MAK della torre antiaerea dell'Arenbergpark, dove nell'ambito del progetto CAT – Contemporary Art Tower si vuole creare una collezione del XXI secolo.

A

MAK – AUSTRIAN MUSEUM OF CONTEMPORARY ARTS

Stubenring 5 // 1st district, Innere Stadt
Tel.: +43 (0)1 711 36-0
www.mak.at

Tue 10 am to midnight, Wed–Sun 10 am to 6 pm
U3 Stubentor

ART 23

MAK DEPOT OF CONTEMPORARY ARTS
GEFECHTSTURM ARENBERGPARK

Dannebergplatz 6 // 3rd district, Landstraße
Tel.: +43 (0)1 711 36-231
www.cat.mak.at

Sun 2 pm to 6 pm (May–Nov)
U3 Rochusgasse

A

SEILERSTÄTTE GALLERIES

Founded in 1971, Gallery Krinzinger is one of the most influential galleries in Austria and with names such as Rudolf Schwarzkogler, Erwin Wurm, Mark Wallinger, and Jonathan Meese, represents some of the most important contemporary Austrian and international artists. Galerie nächst St. Stephan specialized in minimal art, concept art, abstract paintings, installations, and photography/video. Layr Wuestenhagen cultivates young artists whose work—ranging from paintings and photography to object art—reflects internationally relevant themes.

1971 gegründet, zählt die Galerie Krinzinger zu den einflussreichsten Galerien des Landes und vertritt mit Rudolf Schwarzkogler, Erwin Wurm, Mark Wallinger und Jonathan Meese einige der wichtigsten zeitgenössischen österreichischen und internationalen Künstler. Minimal Art, Konzeptkunst, abstrakte Malerei, Installationen und Fotografie/Video prägen das Programm der Galerie nächst St. Stephan. Layr Wuestenhagen fördert vor allem junge Künstler, die von Malerei über Fotografie bis Objektkunst international relevante Themen reflektieren.

ART 25

Fondée en 1971, la galerie Krinzinger est l'une des plus influentes d'Autriche. Elle expose des artistes autrichiens et internationaux contemporains tels qu'Rudolf Schwarzkogler, Erwin Wurm, Mark Wallinger et Jonathan Meese. Art minimal, peinture abstraite, installations et photographie/vidéo sont au programme de la Galerie nächst St. Stephan. Layr Wuestenhagen promeut de jeunes artistes qui s'attèlent à des thèmes pertinents au niveau international : de la peinture à la photographie en passant par l'art conceptuel.

Fondata nel 1971, la Galerie Krinzinger è una delle più prestigiose del Paese. Vi sono rappresentati alcuni dei più importanti artisti contemporanei, austriaci e internazionali, come Rudolf Schwarzkogler, Erwin Wurm, Mark Wallinger e Jonathan Meese. Arte minimalista e concettuale, pittura astratta, installazioni e fotografia/video costituiscono i tratti essenziali della Galerie nächst St. Stephan. La Layr Wuestenhagen promuove giovani artisti che vi espongono opere d'arte concettuale, foto e pitture dedicate a temi di rilevanza internazionale.

LAYR WUESTENHAGEN

An der Hülben 2 // 1st district, Innere Stadt
Tel.: +43 (0)1 524 54 90
www.layrwuestenhagen.com

Tue–Fri 11 am to 6 pm, Sat 11 am to 4 pm
U3 Stubentor

ART 27

NÄCHST ST. STEPHAN R. SCHWARZWÄLDER

Grünangergasse 1/2 //
1st district, Innere Stadt
Tel.: +43 (0)1 512 12 66
www.schwarzwaelder.at

Tue–Fri 11 am to 6 pm,
Sat 11 am to 4 pm
U1, U3 Stephansplatz, U3 Stubentor

KRINZINGER

Seilerstätte 16 // 1st district, Innere Stadt
Tel.: +43 (0)1 513 30 06
www.galerie-krinzinger.at

Tue–Fri noon to 6 pm, Sat 11 am to 4 pm
Tram 1, 2 Weihburggasse

A

THYSSEN-BORNEMISZA ART CONTEMPORARY

Himmelpfortgasse 13 // 1st district, Innere Stadt
Tel.: +43 (0)1 513 98 56-0
www.tba21.org

U1, U3 Stephansplatz

ART 29

As part of its series of projects and exhibitions, Thyssen-Bornemisza Art Contemporary occupies and plays off diverse places and spaces. This is part of the programmed lack of location and strategy of impermanence that the foundation is pursuing. In a palace on the Viennese Himmelpfortgasse, projects, temporary exhibitions from the collection, events, and discussions have been developed and put into practice since April 2004.

Im Rahmen der Projekt- und Ausstellungstätigkeit belegt und bespielt Thyssen-Bornemisza Art Contemporary unterschiedliche Orte und Räume. Die Stiftung verfolgt damit eine programmatische Ortlosigkeit und eine Strategie der Impermanenz. In einem Palais in der Wiener Himmelpfortgasse wurden seit April 2004 Projekte, Wechselausstellungen aus der Sammlung, Veranstaltungen und Diskussionen erarbeitet und realisiert.

Dans le cadre de ses projets et expositions, le Thyssen-Bornemisza Art Contemporary occupe et anime différents lieux et espaces. La fondation propose une programmation nomade et mise sur la stratégie de l'éphémère. Depuis avril 2004, des expositions temporaires issues de la collection et des manifestations ainsi que des discussions sont élaborées et menées à bien dans un palais de l'Himmelpfortgasse.

Per portare avanti i suoi progetti artistici e dare spazio alle esposizioni, la Thyssen-Bornemisza Art Contemporary occupa e gestisce una varietà di spazi e luoghi: la fondazione persegue in questo modo una politica di delocalizzazione programmatica e una strategia dell'impermanenza. Da aprile 2004 è un palazzo di Himmelpfortgasse a Vienna il teatro per l'elaborazione e la realizzazione di progetti artistici, mostre temporanee tratte dall'omonima collezione, manifestazioni e dibattiti.

FRANCE

This collector and producer is also a lateral thinker. Francesca von Habsburg unites the antithetical and the contradictory in interdisciplinary and experimental art projects that are commissioned and presented worldwide. She is giving the name Thyssen-Bornemisza—long a synonym in the art world for the exquisite collection of her family in Madrid—a contemporary identity and has brought her international art patronage to Vienna. This mother of three children has headed up her foundation Thyssen-Bornemisza Art Contemporary (T-B A21), since its founding in 2002; it operates on the cutting edge of fine arts, architecture, music, and performance. The Morning Line, a sound structure commissioned by von Habsburg's foundation, is a work by artist Matthew Ritchie in collaboration with architects Aranda\Lasch and musicians such as Lee Ranaldo (Sonic Youth). It will be presented during the Istanbul 2010 celebrations on the Bosphorus and will move to Vienna in 2011. With an Art Pavilion by Olafur Eliasson and David Adjaye, Francesca von Habsburg has created a stir on the island of Lopud in Croatia for the past three years. The Dalai Lama documentary "The Sun Behind the Clouds" produced by von Habsburg was given the Václav Havel Award in March 2010. Francesca von Habsburg is active in Vienna because "you can work there freely and independently and not be a part of a system that slows you down. Plus, it's a great place to live."

Die Sammlerin und Produzentin gilt als Querdenkerin. Gegensätzliches und Widersprüchliches vereint Francesca von Habsburg in interdisziplinären und experimentellen Kunstprojekten, die weltweit beauftragt und präsentiert werden. Dem Namen Thyssen-Bornemisza – in der Kunstwelt bislang ein Synonym für die exquisite Sammlung ihrer Familie in Madrid – verleiht sie eine zeitgemäße Identität und bringt internationales Mäzenatentum nach Wien. Seit 2002 leitet die Mutter dreier Kinder ihre Stiftung Thyssen-Bornemisza Art Contemporary (T-B A21), die an der Schnittstelle von bildender Kunst, Architektur, Musik und Performance agiert: Die als Auftragswerk entstandene Klangstruktur The Morning Line, ein Werk des Künstlers Matthew Ritchie in Zusammenarbeit mit den Architekten Aranda\Lasch und Musikern wie Lee Ranaldo (Sonic Youth), wird im Rahmen von Istanbul 2010 am Bosporus präsentiert und kommt 2011 nach Wien. Mit einem Pavillon von Olafur Eliasson und David Adjaye setzt Francesca von Habsburg seit drei Jahren Impulse auf der kroatischen Insel Lopud. Die von ihr produzierte Dalai-Lama-Doku „The Sun Behind the Clouds" wurde im März 2010 mit dem Václav-Havel-Preis ausgezeichnet. In Wien ist Francesca von Habsburg aktiv, weil „man dort frei und unabhängig arbeiten kann und nicht Teil eines Systems ist, das einen bremst. Und ich lebe sehr gerne hier".

PORTRAIT 31

SCA VON HABSBURG

Francesca von Habsburg est une collectionneuse d'art et une productrice considérée des moins conformistes, dont les projets artistiques interdisciplinaires et expérimentaux à caractère contradictoire sont mandatés et présentés dans le monde entier. Son nom Thyssen-Bornemisza, qui évoque également la précieuse collection d'art de sa famille à Madrid, lui confère une identité moderne et une position de mécène internationale à Vienne. Mère de trois enfants, elle dirige depuis 2002 sa fondation Thyssen-Bornemisza Art Contemporary, qui se situe à la jonction des beaux-arts, de l'architecture, de la musique et de la performance artistique. L'œuvre mandatée par sa fondation T-B A21, The Morning Line, une installation à identité sonique imaginée par l'artiste Matthew Ritchie en collaboration avec les architectes Aranda\Lasch et des musiciens comme Lee Ranaldo (Sonic Youth), sera présentée au bord du Bosphore lors de l'exposition Istanbul 2010 et à Vienne en 2011. Avec un pavillon conçu par Olafur Eliasson et David Adjaye, Francesca von Habsburg insuffle un vent de création artistique à l'île croate Lopud depuis trois ans. En mars 2010, son documentaire sur le dalaï-lama « The Sun Behind the Clouds » lui a valu le prix Václav Havel. Francesca von Habsburg est très active à Vienne car « on peut travailler ici librement et de manière indépendante, sans être freinée par un système. J'aime vivre dans cette ville ».

Collezionista e produttrice cinematografica dallo spirito alternativo, Francesca von Habsburg unisce elementi opposti e conflittuali in progetti interdisciplinari e sperimentali che vengono commissionati e presentati in tutto il mondo. Al nome Thyssen-Bornemisza – finora adoperato nel mondo dell'arte come sinonimo per la sua prestigiosa collezione di famiglia avente sede a Madrid – Francesca von Habsburg conferisce oggi un'accezione moderna, e ora il nome richiama a Vienna una schiera di mecenati provenienti da ogni parte del mondo. Madre di tre figli, dal 2002 la baronessa presiede la sua fondazione Thyssen-Bornemisza Art Contemporary (T-B A21), che esplora il concatenamento interdisciplinare tra arte, architettura, musica e spettacolo. La struttura acustica The Morning Line, realizzata dall'artista Matthew Ritchie in collaborazione con gli architetti Aranda\Lasch e musicisti come Lee Ranaldo (Sonic Youth), sarà esposta presso il Bosforo in occasione della nomina di Istanbul a Capitale della Cultura Europea 2010, e nel 2011 verrà trasferita a Vienna. Con l'allestimento di un pavilion firmato Olafur Eliasson e David Adjaye, da tre anni Francesca von Habsburg sta dando notevole impulso all'isola croata di Lopud. Nel marzo 2010, il film documentario sul Dalai Lama "The Sun Behind the Clouds", di cui la baronessa è la produttrice esecutiva, ha ottenuto il premio Václav Havel ed opera a Vienna, perché "là si può lavorare liberamente e autonomamente e non si deve sottostare a sistemi che bloccano lo spirito d'iniziativa. E io amo vivere in questa città".

A

ALBERTINA

Albertinaplatz 1 // 1st district, Innere Stadt
Tel.: +43 (0)1 534 83-0
www.albertina.at

Mon–Sun 10 am to 6 pm, Wed 10 am to 9 pm
U1, U2, U4 Karlsplatz/Oper, U1, U3 Stephansplatz

ART 33

The Albertina is home to one of the most important art collections in the world. This museum includes classical modernism works from the Batliner collection, graphic art works ranging from Albrecht Dürer to Andy Warhol, approximately 100,000 photographs, as well as 50,000 architectural drawings and models ranging from Johann Bernhard Fischer von Erlach to Clemens Holzmeister. In 2004, Vienna architect Hans Hollein created a spectacular titanium flying roof to span the entrance to this classical palace.

Die Albertina beherbergt eine der bedeutendsten Kunstsammlungen der Welt, darunter Werke der Klassischen Moderne aus der Sammlung Batliner, grafische Arbeiten von Albrecht Dürer bis Andy Warhol, rund 100 000 Fotografien sowie 50 000 Architekturskizzen und -modelle von Johann Bernhard Fischer von Erlach bis Clemens Holzmeister. 2004 überspannte der Wiener Architekt Hans Hollein den Eingangsbereich des klassizistischen Palais mit einem spektakulären Titan-Flugdach.

L'Albertina abrite l'une des collections d'arts graphiques les plus importantes au monde comptant des œuvres modernes classiques de la collection Batliner, une large palette d'œuvres graphiques allant d'Albrecht Dürer à Andy Warhol, environ 100 000 photographies et 50 000 esquisses architecturales et maquettes d'illustres architectes tels que Johann Bernhard Fischer von Erlach ou Clemens Holzmeister. En 2004, l'architecte viennois Hans Hollein a sublimé le palais classique en dotant son entrée d'un avant-toit prestigieux en titane.

L'Albertina ospita una delle più importanti collezioni d'arte del mondo, comprendente opere del Modernismo Classico provenienti dalla collezione Batliner, capolavori grafici di autori che spaziano da Albrecht Dürer ad Andy Warhol, circa 100 000 foto e 50 000 disegni e modelli architettonici che portano la firma di artisti quali Johann Bernhard Fischer von Erlach e Clemens Holzmeister. Nel 2004 il viennese Hans Hollein ha arricchito la zona d'ingresso di questo palazzo in stile neoclassico con uno spettacolare tetto in titanio a forma d'ala.

ESCHENBACHGASSE GALLERIES

A lively gallery scene has developed on Eschenbachgasse. Gallery Krobath specializes in space-related works, new media and current trends in painting, while Martin Janda introduces contemporary concept art, paintings, drawings, films/videos, and sculptures and installations. Meyer Kainer features established artists such as Franz West or Yoshitomo Nara and cultivates young artists such as Gelitin. Gallery Steinek specializes in photography, contextual paintings, video, and object art.

In der Eschenbachgasse hat sich eine rege Galerienszene entwickelt. Während sich die Galerie Krobath auf raumbezogene Arbeiten, neue Medien und aktuelle Tendenzen in der Malerei konzentriert, präsentiert Martin Janda zeitgenössische Konzeptkunst, Malerei, Zeichnung, Film/Video, Skulptur und Installation. Meyer Kainer betreut etablierte Künstler wie Franz West oder Yoshitomo Nara und fördert junge Künstler wie Gelitin. Die Schwerpunkte der Galerie Steinek liegen auf Fotografie, kontextueller Malerei, Video und Objektkunst.

ART 35

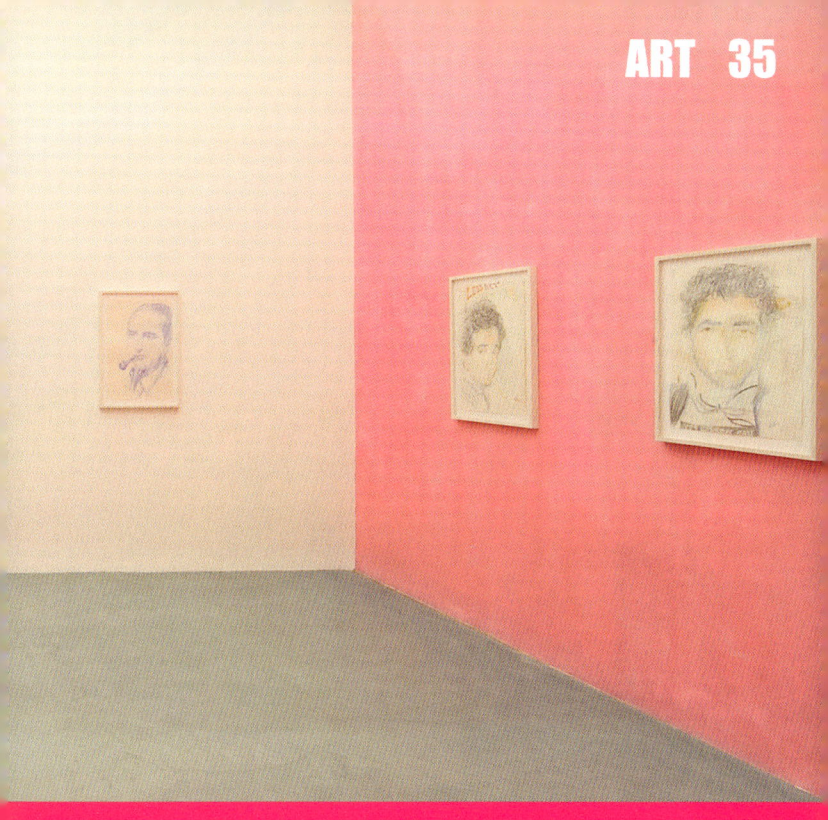

Cette ruelle regorge de galeries d'art. Alors que la galerie Krobath est axée sur les travaux concentrés sur l'espace, les nouveaux médias et les tendances actuelles en peinture, la galerie Martin Janda expose de l'art conceptuel contemporain, de la peinture, du dessin, des films, de la sculpture et des installations. Meyer Kainer accompagne des artistes établis comme Franz West ou Yoshitomo Nara et encourage de jeunes artistes comme Gelitin. La galerie Steinek est spécialisée dans la photographie, la peinture contextuelle, la vidéo et l'art conceptuel.

In Eschenbachgasse è sorto un vivace panorama artistico costellato di gallerie. Mentre la Galerie Krobath si concentra su opere a tema specifico, nuovi media e attuali tendenze nella pittura, la Martin Janda presenta arte concettuale, dipinti, disegni, film, sculture e installazioni d'epoca contemporanea. Nella Meyer Kainer trovano spazio artisti affermati quali Franz West e Yoshitomo Nara, ma si promuovono anche giovani talenti come Gelitin. La Galerie Steinek è invece dedicata a fotografia, pittura contestuale, video e arte oggettuale.

A

KROBATH

Eschenbachgasse 9 //
1st district, Innere Stadt
Tel.: +43 (0)1 585 74 70
www.galeriekrobath.at

Tue–Fri 1 pm to 6 pm,
Sat 11 am to 3 pm
U2 Museumsquartier

MARTIN JANDA

Eschenbachgasse 11 //
1st district, Innere Stadt
Tel.: +43 (0)1 585 73 71
www.martinjanda.at

Tue–Fri 1 am to 6 pm,
Sat 11 am to 3 pm
U2 Museumsquartier

ART 37

MEYER KAINER

Eschenbachgasse 9 //
1st district, Innere Stadt
Tel.: +43 (0)1 585 72 77
www.meyerkainer.com

Tue–Fri 12 am to 7 pm,
Sat 11 am to 4 pm
U2 Museumsquartier

STEINEK

Eschenbachgasse 4 //
1st district, Innere Stadt
Tel.: + 43 (0)1 512 87 59
galerie.steinek.at

Tue–Fri 1 pm to 6 pm,
Sat 11 am to 3 pm
U2 Museumsquartier

A

MUSEUMSQUARTIER

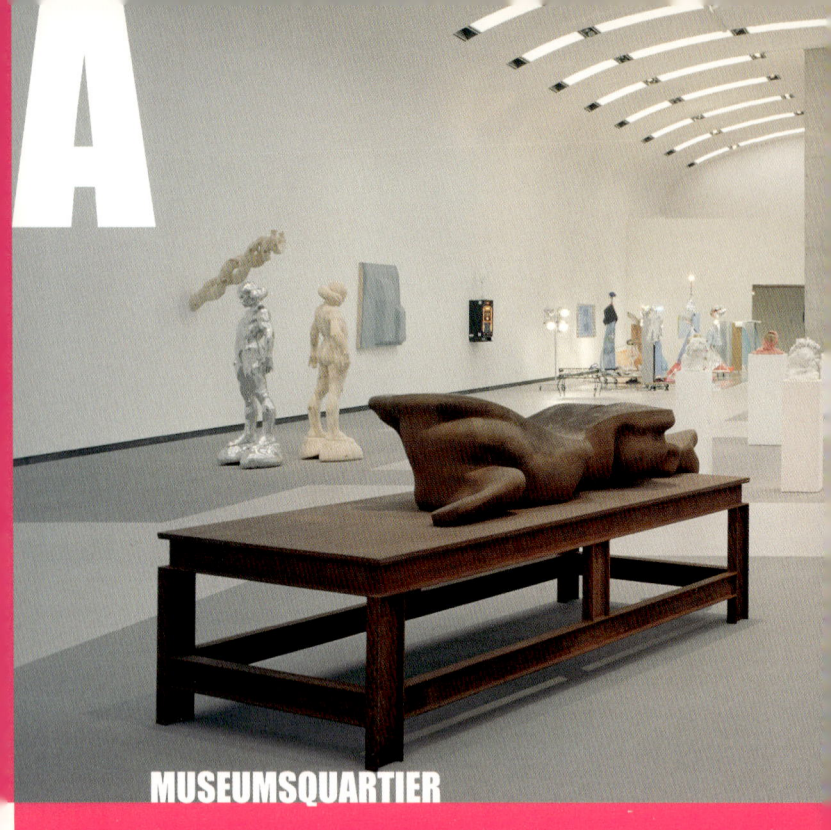

Designed by architects Ortner & Ortner and Manfred Wehdorn and opened in 2001, the 15-acre MuseumsQuartier on the grounds of the former imperial stables provides space for modern and contemporary art and culture. Options range from large art museums such as the Leopold Museum and the MUMOK to contemporary art exhibition spaces like KUNSTHALLE wien to Tanzquartier Wien (center for contemporary dance), Architekturzentrum Wien, and quartier21, the "creative cluster."

Seit 2001 bietet das von den Architekten Ortner & Ortner und Manfred Wehdorn konzipierte MuseumsQuartier auf 60 000 m² auf dem Gelände der ehemaligen Kaiserlichen Hofstallungen Raum für moderne und zeitgenössische Kunst und Kultur. Das Angebot reicht von großen Kunstmuseen wie dem Leopold Museum und dem MUMOK über Ausstellungsräume für zeitgenössische Kunst wie der KUNSTHALLE wien bis zum Tanzquartier Wien, dem Architekturzentrum Wien und dem „Creative Cluster" quartier21.

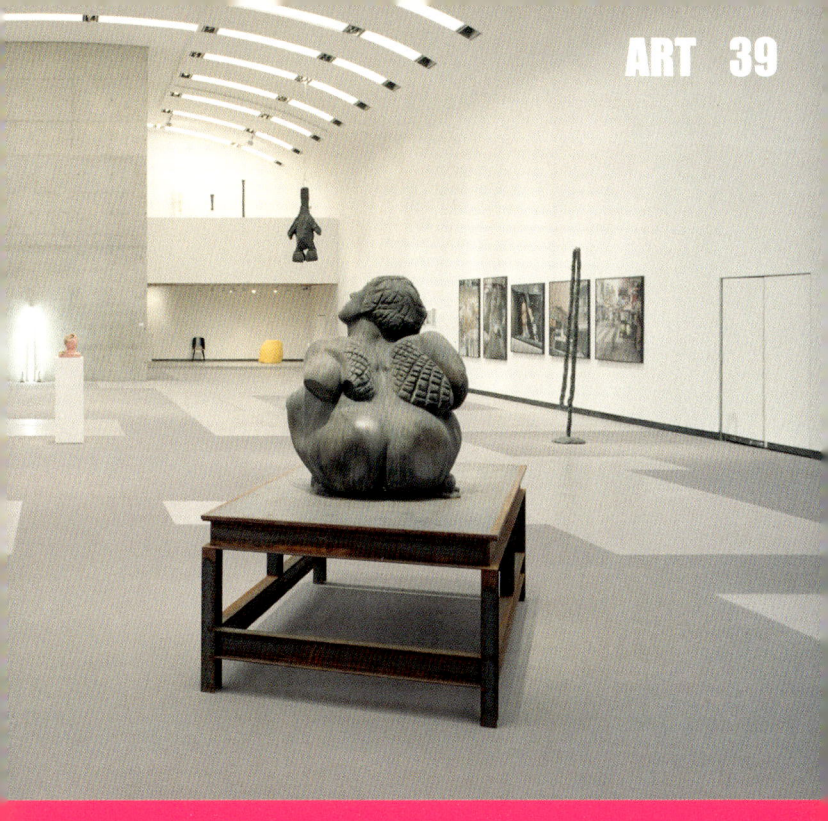

ART 39

Depuis 2001, le MuseumsQuartier, pensé par les architectes Ortner & Ortner et Manfred Wehdorn, fait la part belle à l'art moderne et contemporain et la culture sur une surface de 60 000 m^2, dans les anciennes écuries impériales. Il regroupe entre autres de grands musées d'art comme le Leopold Museum et le MUMOK, des salles d'exposition dédiées à l'art contemporain comme la KUNSTHALLE wien, le Tanzquartier Wien (centre voué à la danse contemporaine), l'Architekturzentrum Wien et un « creative cluster », le quartier 21.

Realizzato dagli architetti Ortner & Ortner e Manfred Wehdorn dove un tempo sorgeva il palazzo delle scuderie dell'imperatore, il MuseumsQuartier riunisce su una superficie di 60 000 m^2 arte e cultura moderna e contemporanea. L'offerta spazia da grandi musei come il Leopold Museum e il MUMOK a sale espositive per opere d'arte contemporanea come la KUNSTHALLE wien, passando per il Tanzquartier Wien (centro di danza contemporanea), l'Architekturzentrum Wien e il "creative cluster" quartier21.

A

MUMOK – MUSEUM MODERNER KUNST STIFTUNG LUDWIG WIEN

MuseumsQuartier, Museumsplatz 1 // 7th district, Neubau
Tel.: +43 (0)1 525 00
www.mumok.at

Mon–Sun 10 am to 6 pm, Thu 10 am to 9 pm
U2 Museumsquartier, U2, U3 Volkstheater

ART 41

KUNSTHALLE WIEN

MuseumsQuartier, Museumsplatz 1 // 7th district, Neubau
Tel.: +43 (0)1 521 89-0
www.kunsthallewien.at

Mon–Sun 10 am to 7 pm, Thu 10 am to 9 pm
U2 Museumsquartier, U2, U3 Volkstheater

A

LEOPOLD MUSEUM

MuseumsQuartier, Museumsplatz 1 // 7th district, Neubau
Tel.: +43 (0)1 525 70-0
www.leopoldmuseum.org

Mon, Wed–Sun 10 am to 6 pm, Thu 10 am to 9 pm
U2 Museumsquartier, U2, U3 Volkstheater

ART 43

TANZQUARTIER WIEN

MuseumsQuartier, Museumsplatz 1 // 7th district, Neubau
Tel.: +43 (0)1 581 35 91
www.tqw.at

Mon–Sat 9 am to 8 pm
U2 Museumsquartier, U2, U3 Volkstheater

A

Mocked by contemporaries at the end of the 19th century for its golden dome and for its simple and unadorned architecture, the Secession building designed by Joseph Maria Olbrich is now considered to be one of the key works of the Jugendstil movement in Vienna. The Beethoven Frieze, painted by Gustav Klimt in 1902, is on display in the basement of the building, while the ground floor houses changing exhibitions by contemporary artists such as Doug Aitken, Sharon Lockhart or Terence Koh.

Ende des 19. Jahrhunderts von den Zeitgenossen wegen der für damals allzu schlichten Architektur und der vergoldeten Kuppel noch mit Spott bedacht, gilt die von Joseph Maria Olbrich erbaute Secession heute als eines der Schlüsselwerke des Wiener Jugendstils. Im Untergeschoss ist der 1902 von Gustav Klimt geschaffene Beethovenfries zu besichtigen, im Erdgeschoss werden Wechselausstellungen zeitgenössischer Künstler wie Doug Aitken, Sharon Lockhart oder Terence Koh gezeigt.

Le Palais de la Sécession, construit à la fin du XIXe siècle par Jospeh Maria Olbrich, et qui fut à l'époque très raillé à cause de son architecture jugée trop sobre et de son dôme doré, est aujourd'hui considéré comme une œuvre clé de l'Art nouveau viennois. Dans la salle du sous-sol, vous pourrez admirer la Frise Beethoven réalisée en 1902 par Gustav Klimt. Au rez-de-chaussée, des expositions temporaires d'artistes comme Doug Aitken, Sharon Lockhart ou Terence Koh sont proposées.

Alla fine del XIX secolo era ancora deriso dai critici contemporanei a causa della linea architettonica troppo semplice per i canoni di allora e la cupola dorata, mentre oggi il palazzo, progettato da Joseph Maria Olbrich, rappresenta una delle opere architettoniche più emblematiche dello Jugendstil viennese. Al piano inferiore si può ammirare il fregio di Beethoven realizzato nel 1902 da Gustav Klimt, mentre al pianterreno sono allestite mostre temporanee dedicate ad artisti dei giorni nostri quali Doug Aitken, Sharon Lockhart e Terence Koh.

ART 45

SECESSION

Friedrichstraße 12 // 1st district, Innere Stadt
Tel.: +43 (0)1 587 53 07
www.secession.at

Tue–Sun 10 am to 6 pm
U1, U2, U4 Karlsplatz/Oper

A

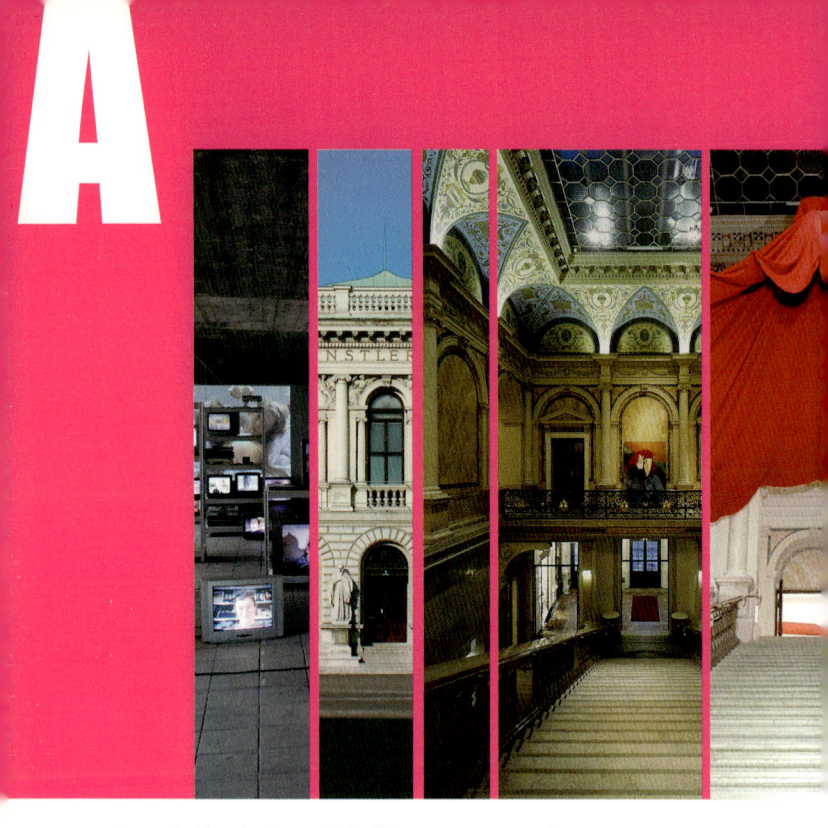

A 22,000-sq.-ft. historic Ringstraße building, the Künstlerhaus hosts exhibitions relating to architecture and interdisciplinary themes, international cooperations, and exhibitions for artist association members. The passage gallery at the subway entrance is an experimentation lab for young artists. Across the way, the Wien Museum Karlsplatz specializes in the history of the city as well as Vienna's art, fashion and everyday culture. One highlight from the permanent exhibition is the living room from the apartment of legendary architect Adolf Loos.

Auf 2 000 m² zeigt das in einem historischen Ringstraßenbau beheimatete Künstlerhaus Ausstellungen zu Architektur und interdisziplinären Themen, internationale Kooperationen sowie Präsentationen der Mitglieder des Künstlervereins. Die Passagegalerie am U-Bahn-Abgang dient jungen Künstlern als Experimentierfeld. Das gegenüberliegende Wien Museum Karlsplatz widmet sich neben der Stadtgeschichte auch Wiens Kunst, Mode und Alltagskultur. Ein Highlight ist das Wohnzimmer aus der Wohnung des legendären Architekten Adolf Loos.

ART 47

KÜNSTLERHAUS – K/HAUS

Karlsplatz 5 // 1st district, Innere Stadt
Tel.: +43 (0)1 587 96 63
www.k-haus.at

Mon–Sun 10 am to 6 pm,
Thu 10 am to 9 pm
U1, U2, U4 Karlsplatz/Oper

WIEN MUSEUM KARLSPLATZ

Karlsplatz // 4th district, Wieden
Tel.: +43 (0)1 505 87 47-0
www.wienmuseum.at

Tue–Sun 10 am to 6 pm
U1, U2, U4 Karlsplatz/Oper

Dans un bâtiment historique de 2 000 m² de la Ringstraße, la Künstlerhaus dévoile des expositions sur l'architecture, des thèmes pluridisciplinaires, des coopérations internationales et des présentations des membres de l'association d'artistes. La galerie du passage à la sortie du métro sert de terrain d'expérimentation aux jeunes artistes. En face, le Wien Museum Karlsplatz est consacré à l'histoire de la ville, l'art, la mode et l'art de vivre à la viennoise. Le bijou de l'exposition permanente est le salon de l'appartement de l'architecte Adolf Loos.

Ospitata in un edificio storico vicino a Ringstraße, la Künstlerhaus dedica 2 000 m² a mostre su architettura e temi interdisciplinari, cooperazioni internazionali e presentazioni degli esponenti dell'associazione artistica. La galleria nel sottopassaggio vicino alla discesa della metropolitana funge da spazio sperimentale per giovani artisti. Il Wien Museum Karlsplatz, di fronte, copre la storia della città ma anche l'arte, la moda e lo stile di vita di Vienna. Nella mostra permanente spicca il salotto appartenuto al mitico architetto Adolf Loos.

A

BELVEDERE

ART 49

A

BELVEDERE

Oberes Belvedere
Prinz-Eugen-Straße 27 //
3rd district, Landstraße
Tel.: +43 (0)1 795 57-0

Mon–Sun 10 am to 6 pm
U1 Südtirolerplatz,
Tram D Schloss Belvedere,
Tram 18 Südbahnhof

Unteres Belvedere + Orangerie
Rennweg 6 // 3rd district, Landstraße
Tel.: +43 (0)1 795 57-0
www.belvedere.at

Mon–Sun 10 am to 6 pm,
Wed 10 am to 9 pm
Tram 71 Unteres Belvedere

Agnes Husslein-Arco spearheaded the effort to revamp the collections of the Belvedere with significant works by Gustav Klimt, Egon Schiele, and Oskar Kokoschka presented in the Upper Belvedere. The Lower Belvedere, and Orangery house special exhibitions relating to Austrian art in an international context; since 2009, the two structures have been connected by a steel and glass corridor designed by Berlin architects Kuehn Malvezzi and cleverly integrated into the Baroque architecture. The Kammergarten contains sculptures by Alfred Hrdlicka, Franz West and Dan Graham.

Unter der Direktion von Agnes Husslein-Arco wurden die Sammlungen des Belvedere mit bedeutenden Werken von Gustav Klimt, Egon Schiele und Oskar Kokoschka im Oberen Belvedere neu aufgestellt. Hochkarätige Sonderausstellungen zu österreichischer Kunst im internationalen Kontext werden im Unteren Belvedere und der Orangerie präsentiert, die seit 2009 durch einen sensibel in die Barockarchitektur integrierten Stahl-Glas-Korridor der Berliner Architekten Kuehn Malvezzi verbunden sind. Im Kammergarten sind Skulpturen von Alfred Hrdlicka, Franz West und Dan Graham zu sehen.

La présentation des collections du Belvédère supérieur comptant d'importantes œuvres de Gustav Klimt, Egon Schiele et Oskar Kokoschka a été repensée par Agnes Husslein-Arco. Le Belvédère inférieur et l'Orangerie présentent des expositions temporaires sur l'art autrichien. Ces deux bâtiments sont reliés depuis 2009 par un couloir d'acier et de verre habilement intégré à l'architecture baroque par l'architecte berlinois Kuehn Malvezzi. Les jardins arborent des sculptures de Alfred Hrdlicka, Franz West et Dan Graham.

Sotto la guida di Agnes Husslein-Arco, le collezioni del Belvedere Superiore sono state riorganizzate con l'inserimento di importanti opere di Gustav Klimt, Egon Schiele ed Oskar Kokoschka. Prestigiose mostre dedicate all'arte austriaca trovano spazio invece nel Belvedere Inferiore e nell'Orangerie, unita al palazzo da un corridoio in vetro e acciaio realizzato nel 2009 dagli architetti Kuehn Malvezzi in perfetta linea con lo stile barocco della costruzione. Nel giardino si possono ammirare sculture di Alfred Hrdlicka, Franz West e Dan Graham.

SCHLEIFMÜHLGASSE GALLERIES

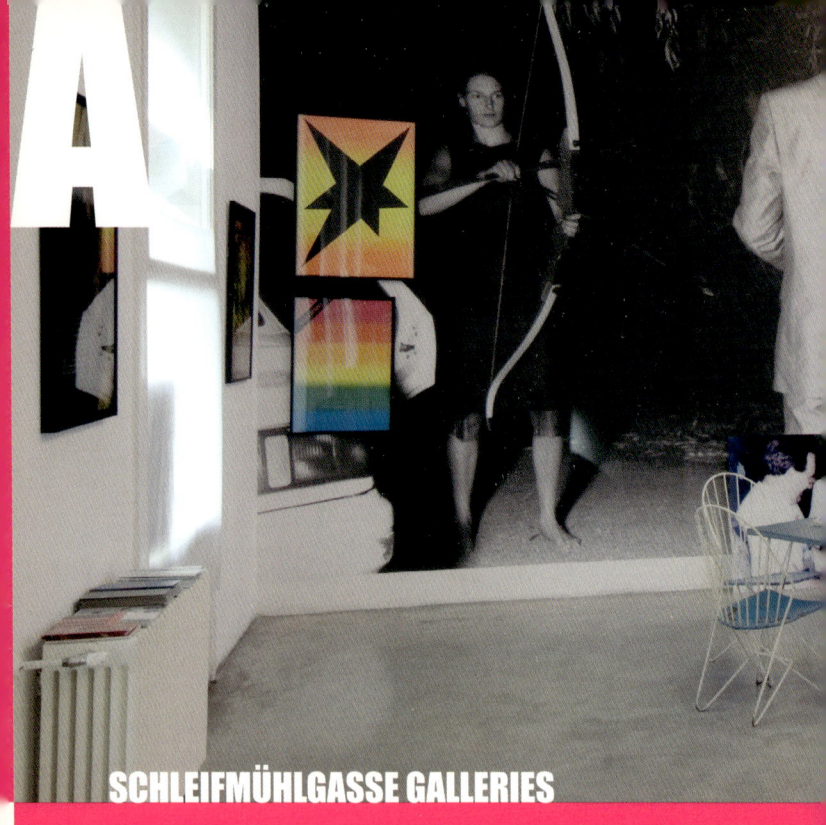

Galleries Senn, König, Engholm, and Kargl on Schleifmühlgasse all showcase contemporary art with a strong international focus. These galleries often coordinate exhibitions and have established themselves as fixtures in Vienna's cultural life. Represented artists include Hans Weigand, Cosima von Bonin, and Marko Lulic at Senn, G.R.A.M. and Pierre Bismuth at Christine König, Hans Schabus and Constanze Ruhm at Engholm, and Markus Schinwald and Mark Dion at Kargl.

Zeitgenössische Kunst mit starker internationaler Ausrichtung präsentieren die Galerien Senn, König, Engholm und Kargl in der Schleifmühlgasse, oft mit gemeinsamen Vernissageterminen, die sich als Fixpunkte im Wiener Kulturleben etabliert haben. Zu den vertretenen Künstlern zählen Hans Weigand, Cosima von Bonin und Marko Lulic bei Senn, G.R.A.M. und Pierre Bismuth bei Christine König, Hans Schabus und Constanze Ruhm bei Engholm sowie Markus Schinwald und Mark Dion bei Kargl.

ART 53

Les galeries Senn, König, Engholm et Kargl de la Schleifmühlgasse exposent de l'art contemporain à forte orientation internationale. Les vernissages de ces galeries, souvent planifiés aux mêmes dates, sont désormais des incontournables de la vie culturelle viennoise. Parmi les artistes représentés, on compte Hans Weigand, Cosima von Bonin et Marko Lulic chez Senn, G.R.A.M. et Pierre Bismuth chez Christine König, Hans Schabus et Constanze Ruhm chez Engholm ainsi que Markus Schinwald et Mark Dion chez Kargl.

Le gallerie Senn, König, Engholm e Kargl di Schleifmühlgasse presentano mostre d'arte contemporanea con un forte orientamento al contesto internazionale, spesso corredate da vernissage allestite contemporaneamente nelle varie sedi che sono ormai diventate capisaldi del panorama culturale viennese. Tra gli artisti rappresentati figurano Hans Weigand, Cosima von Bonin e Marko Lulic presso la Senn, G.R.A.M. e Pierre Bismuth alla Christine König, Hans Schabus e Constanze Ruhm nell'Engholm e Markus Schinwald e Mark Dion alla Kargl.

A

CHRISTINE KÖNIG

Schleifmühlgasse 1A //
4th district, Wieden
Tel.: +43 (0)1 585 74 74
www.christinekoeniggalerie.com

Tue–Fri 11 am to 7 pm,
Sat 11 am to 3 pm
Tram 1, 62 Paulanergasse, bus 59A Schleifmühlgasse

ENGHOLM

Schleifmühlgasse 3 //
4th district, Wieden
Tel.: +43 (0)1 585 73 37
www.kerstinengholm.com

Tue–Fri 11 am to 6 pm, Sat 11 am to 3 pm

ART 55

GABRIELE SENN

Schleifmühlgasse 1A //
4th district, Wieden
Tel.: +43 (0)1 585 25 80
www.galeriesenn.at

Tue–Fri 11 am to 6 pm,
Sat 11 am to 3 pm

GEORG KARGL FINE ARTS

Schleifmühlgasse 5 //
4th district, Wieden
Tel.: +43 (0)1 585 41 99
www.georgkargl.com

Tue–Fri 11 am to 7 pm, Thu 11 am to 8 pm,
Sat 11 am to 3 pm

A

Subtly redesigned by architects Eichinger oder Knechtl, this 1950s-era loft has housed the first large-scale photography gallery in Austria since it opened in 2001. Aside from a permanent exhibition of approximately 800 historic cameras ranging from the first Leica to the AEG sky imager, the WestLicht gallery also provides space for changing exhibitions of noted photographic artists such as Nobuyoshi Araki, Thomas Hoepker, or Herbert List as well as space for group shows of up-and-coming photographers.

Seit 2001 beherbergt das von den Architekten Eichinger oder Knechtl subtil umgearbeitete 50er-Jahre-Loft den ersten großen „Schauplatz für Fotografie" in Österreich. Neben der aus etwa 800 historischen Kameras bestehenden, von der ersten Leica bis zur AEG Wolkenkamera reichenden, permanenten Schausammlung, bietet das WestLicht Raum für etwa alle zwei Monate wechselnde Ausstellungen renommierter Fotokünstler wie Nobuyoshi Araki, Thomas Hoepker oder Herbert List sowie für Gruppenshows aufstrebender junger Fotografen.

Depuis 2001, ce loft des années 50, remanié par le cabinet d'architectes Eichinger oder Knechtl, abrite la plus grande « vitrine de la photographie » en Autriche. En plus de l'exposition permanente composée de quelque 800 appareils photo, WestLicht propose des expositions temporaires renouvelées environ tous les deux mois. Des photographes renommés tels que Nobuyoshi Araki, Thomas Hoepker ou Herbert List y présentent leurs œuvres. WestLicht permet également à de jeunes photographes de faire des expositions groupées.

Questo loft degli anni '50, sapientemente ristrutturato dagli architetti Eichinger oder Knechtl, ospita dal 2001 il più grande "palcoscenico per la fotografia" dell'Austria. Accanto alle esposizioni permanenti, composte da circa 800 apparecchi fotografici (dalla prima Leica alla fotocamera satellitare AEG), il museo WestLicht dà spazio a mostre temporanee che cambiano ogni due mesi dedicate a fotografi come Nobuyoshi Araki, Thomas Hoepker e Herbert List, ma ospita anche rassegne collettive di foto scattate da giovani artisti promettenti.

ART 57

WESTLICHT

Westbahnstraße 40 // 7th district, Neubau
Tel.: +43 (0)1 522 66 36
www.westlicht.com

Tue, Wed, Fri 2 pm to 7 pm, Thu 2 pm to 9 pm,
Sat+Sun 11 am to 7 pm
Tram 5 Westbahnstraße, 49 Kaiserstraße

A

Designed by architect Heinz Tesar, the Essl Museum has housed the extensive collection of Karlheinz and Agnes Essl since 1999. This collection includes significant works from representatives of Austrian Modernism, Vienna Actionism and the Neue Wilde movements, as well as individual pieces from artists such as Maria Lassnig or Valie Export who are presented within the context of international contemporary art. The emerging artists series and the biennial Essl Award support young artists.

Seit 1999 beherbergt das von dem Architekten Heinz Tesar entworfene Essl Museum die umfangreiche Sammlung von Karlheinz und Agnes Essl. Diese umfasst bedeutende Werke der österreichischen Moderne, des Wiener Aktionismus, der Neuen Wilden und Einzelpositionen wie Maria Lassnig oder Valie Export, die im Kontext internationaler zeitgenössischer Kunst präsentiert werden. Die Reihe „emerging artists" und der alle zwei Jahre vergebene Essl Award unterstützen junge Kunst.

Depuis 1999, le musée Essl, dessiné par l'architecte Heinz Tesar, abrite l'importante collection de Karlheinz et Agnes Essl. Elle regroupe des œuvres marquantes de l'art moderne autrichien, du Wiener Aktionismus (Actionnisme viennois), de la Neue Wilde (Les nouveaux fauves) et des œuvres d'artistes comme Maria Lassnig ou Valie Export présentées dans le contexte de l'art contemporain international. La série d'expositions « emergin artists » et l'Essl Award décerné tous les deux ans encouragent les jeunes artistes.

Progettato dall'architetto Heinz Tesar, dal 1999 l'Essl Museum è la sede della ricca collezione di Karlheinz e Agnes Essl, che comprende importanti opere del Modernismo austriaco, dell'Azionismo viennese, dei Nuovi Selvaggi e vetrine individuali dedicate ad artisti quali Maria Lassnig o Valie Export, il tutto presentato nel contesto dell'arte contemporanea internazionale. La rassegna "emerging artists" e il premio Essl Award, assegnato ogni due anni, sono iniziative volte a sostenere i giovani artisti.

ART 59

ESSL MUSEUM

An der Donau-Au 1
3400 Klosterneuburg bei Wien
Tel.: +43 (0)2243 370 50-150
www.essl.museum

Tue–Sun 10 am to 6 pm, Wed 10 am to 9 pm
Free shuttle bus from Albertinaplatz to Essl Museum

ARCHIT

A

It's understandable that well-known architectural highlights such as the Gothic St. Stephen's Cathedral or the Baroque Schönbrunn Palace attract many visitors, and the city has examples of probably every architectural style in European history. Off the beaten track, however, you can also discover exciting architecture from the more recent past and the present, ranging from Otto Wagner's Jugendstil buildings to numerous examples of modern architecture. Back at the turn of the 20th century, there was a unique phase of architectural creativity in Vienna unlike anywhere else in the world, and after World War I the city made important strides in public housing. In the second half of the 20th century, Austrian architects with international standing such as Roland Rainer, Helmut Richter, Günter Domenig, Hans Hollein, or Coop Himmelb(l)au have left their mark on the city, but international architects have been brought in as well: Dominique Perrault will shortly begin construction on two skyscrapers, and Jean Nouvel just finished his building along the Danube Canal. With architects such as Zaha Hadid and Hitoshi Abe participating in the construction of Vienna's new University of Economics and Business campus, we are again seeing high-quality, cutting-edge architecture appearing in Vienna.

Natürlich locken bekannte architektonische Highlights wie der gotische Stephansdom oder das barocke Schloss Schönbrunn viele Besucher an, und die Stadt bietet Begegnungen mit wohl allen Baustilen der europäischen Geschichte. Abseits davon kann man aber, von den Jugendstilbauten Otto Wagners bis zur aktuellen Baukunst, spannende Architektur der jüngeren Vergangenheit und Gegenwart entdecken. Um die vorletzte Jahrhundertwende gab es in Wien eine weltweit einzigartige Phase architektonischer Kreativität, nach dem Ersten Weltkrieg gingen von der Stadt wichtige Impulse im sozialen Wohnbau aus. Seit der zweiten Hälfte des 20. Jahrhunderts haben österreichische Architekten mit Weltgeltung wie Roland Rainer, Helmut Richter, Günter Domenig, Hans Hollein oder Coop Himmelb(l)au in der Stadt ihre Zeichen gesetzt, aber auch internationale Architekten wurden geholt: Dominique Perrault baut demnächst einen Zwillingsturm, Jean Nouvel hat gerade ein Hotel am Donaukanal vollendet. Und mit dem Bau des neuen WU-Campus, an dem Architekten wie Zaha Hadid und Hitoshi Abe maßgeblich beteiligt sind, entsteht nun auch in Wien wieder qualitätsvolle, zukunftsweisende Architektur.

INTRO ARCHITECTURE 63

De toute évidence, des chefs d'œuvre architectoniques comme le Stephansdom de style gothique ou le château Schönbrunn de style baroque attirent une kyrielle de visiteurs et la ville propose un vaste éventail d'œuvres de tous les styles de l'histoire européenne. On peut également y découvrir un éventail architectural allant des édifices Art nouveau d'Otto Wagner aux courants actuels, ainsi qu'une architecture d'un passé récent et de l'époque actuelle. Au tournant de l'avant-dernier siècle, Vienne fut le théâtre d'une vague de créations architectoniques. Après la première guerre mondiale, la ville connut un véritable essor urbain avec la construction de logements sociaux. À partir de la deuxième moitié du XXe siècle, des architectes autrichiens de renommée mondiale comme Roland Rainer, Helmut Richter, Günter Domenig, Hans Hollein ou Coop Himmelb(l)au y ont laissé leurs empruntes. Mais on y trouve également des œuvres d'architectes étrangers, comme les tours jumelles de Dominique Perrault et l'édifice de Jean Nouvel sur le canal du Danube. Le nouveau bâtiment du campus de l'université d'économie de Vienne, conçu par les architectes Zaha Hadid et Hitoshi Abe, reflète à son tour une architecture futuriste et de qualité.

Certo, le più famose attrattive architettoniche viennesi come il duomo gotico di Santo Stefano o il castello barocco di Schönbrunn richiamano molti visitatori, inoltre la città offre esempi di forse tutti gli stili architettonici della storia europea. A parte ciò, tuttavia, nella capitale austriaca si possono scoprire anche capolavori architettonici del passato più recente e dei giorni nostri, dalle costruzioni in stile Jugendstil di Otto Wagner all'arte edilizia contemporanea. A cavallo tra il XIX e XX secolo Vienna conobbe un periodo di fioritura in campo architettonico paragonabile a nessun altro luogo al mondo, e dopo la prima Guerra Mondiale la città diede notevole impulso al settore dell'edilizia abitativa sociale. A partire dalla seconda metà del XX secolo, architetti austriaci di fama mondiale come Roland Rainer, Helmut Richter, Günter Domenig, Hans Hollein e Coop Himmelb(l)au hanno lasciato la loro inconfondibile impronta nella città, dove tuttavia sono approdati anche architetti internazionali: Dominique Perrault costruirà prossimamente una torre a due punte, mentre Jean Nouvel ha appena ultimato la propria opera sul Canale del Danubio. E con la costruzione del nuovo campus dell'Università di Scienze Economiche, in cui hanno avuto un ruolo determinante architetti come Zaha Hadid e Hitoshi Abe, fa ora capolino anche a Vienna, ancora una volta, architettura di prestigio e d'avanguardia.

A

DIE BREMER STADTMUSIKANTEN

Tokiostraße 6 // 22nd district, Donaustadt

Bus 27A Arakawastraße (via U1 Kagran),
Tram 26 Donaufelder Straße/Josef-Baumann-Gasse

ARCHITECTURE 65

Grimm's fairy tale of the Bremen Town Musicians inspired ARTEC's terraced housing complex on Tokiostraße: Just like the four animals in the fairy tale, here apartments of different sizes are stacked on top of each other—studios with an open loft and terrace on the ground floor, then multi-level apartments facing an inner courtyard, then classic terraced houses, and finally garden sheds. The roof has a swimming pool with a sun deck, and playgrounds for kids and adults are located at mid-level and in the landscaped ground-level courtyard.

Grimms Märchen von den Bremer Stadtmusikanten inspirierte ARTEC Architekten zu ihrem Terrassenhaus in der Tokiostraße: Wie die Märchentiere Hahn, Katze, Hund und Esel liegen hier unterschiedlich große Wohngebäude gestapelt übereinander – Lofts mit Galerie und Garten im Erdgeschoss, darüber Maisonetten mit Atrium, darauf Reihenhäuser und zuoberst urbane Kleingartenhäuschen. Auf dem Dach gibt es ein Schwimmbecken mit Sonnenterrasse, auf halber Höhe und im begrünten Innenhof liegen Spielplätze für Kinder und Erwachsene.

Le bureau d'architectes ARTEC, s'est inspiré des « Musiciens de Brème », le conte de Grimm, pour réaliser la maison à terrasses. Comme les animaux du conte, de grandes unités d'habitation de différentes dimensions sont superposées : des lofts avec galerie et jardin au rez-de-chaussée, des mezzanines avec patio au-dessus, des maisons mitoyennes encore au-dessus et des petites cabanes de jardin de style urbain tout en haut. Il y a une piscine avec terrasse ensoleillée sur le toit mais aussi une cour avec terrains de jeux.

Per la costruzione dell'edificio a più livelli di Tokiostraße, lo studio di architetti ARTEC si è ispirato alla fiaba dei fratelli Grimm "I musicanti di Brema". Come nella favola il gallo, il gatto, il cane e l'asino, qui unità abitative di varia grandezza sono disposte una sopra l'altra: loft con soppalco e giardino al piano terra, sopra maisonette con atrio, ancora sopra case a schiera e all'ultimo livello pergolati. Sul tetto c'è una piscina con solarium, a metà altezza e nel verdeggiante cortile interno aree giochi per bambini e adulti.

A

WOHNBAU SPITTELAU

Spittelauer Lände 10 // 9th district, Alsergrund

U4, U6 Spittelau

ARCHITECTURE 67

Zaha Hadid's only finished building in Vienna to date is a housing project straddling Otto Wagner's historic viaduct. The project was intended to enhance the value of the area surrounding the Vienna waste incineration plant and provide space for apartments and small businesses but has been criticized as being asymmetrical and skewed. The concept of using a deconstructive architectural style to accommodate the requirements of public housing fell flat. This building is currently being used by international student organizations.

Zaha Hadids bisher einziges fertiggestelltes Wiener Projekt ist eine Wohnanlage, die auf denkmalgeschützten Stadtbahnbögen von Otto Wagner sitzt. Der asymmetrische, als windschief kritisierte Bau sollte die Gegend um die Wiener Müllverbrennungsanlage aufwerten und Wohnungen und Geschäftslokale enthalten. Das Konzept, eine dekonstruktivistische Architektur mit den Erfordernissen des sozialen Wohnungsbaus in Einklang zu bringen, ging nicht auf. Aktuell nutzen es internationale Studentenvereinigungen.

Ce projet de Zaha Hadid est un complexe immobilier juché sur les arcades de métro d'Otto Wagner classées monument historique. Ce bâtiment asymétrique controversé à cause de sa forme de travers, a été construit pour revaloriser le quartier proche de l'incinérateur d'ordures et accueillir des appartements et commerces. Le projet ayant pour but d'allier une architecture déconstructiviste aux besoins d'un immeuble d'habitation social ne s'est jamais réalisé. Actuellement, il est utilisé par des associations étudiantes internationales.

L'unica opera finora realizzata da Zaha Hadid a Vienna è un edificio residenziale sopra il viadotto della metropolitana di Otto Wagner, salvaguardato come patrimonio culturale. Questa struttura asimmetrica, definita "sghemba", è nata con lo scopo di valorizzare la zona intorno all'inceneritore di Vienna e contenere appartamenti e locali ad uso commerciale. L'idea di fondere una linea architettonica decostruttiva con le esigenze di un complesso residenziale sociale non è andata a buon fine, e oggi la struttura è sede di associazioni studentesche internazionali.

A

Albert Wimmer's redesign of the Wien Praterstern train station took a rundown structure cobbled together over the years and replaced it with a uniform building topped by a transparent roof to brighten the spacious interior and provide easier access to the platforms. The facade incorporates inset elements that both reflect sunlight or the lights of surrounding buildings at night, and lend an inviting air to the Boris Podrecca-designed courtyard. Wimmer has also been commissioned with the new construction of the Vienna central station.

Albert Wimmers Neugestaltung des Bahnhofs Wien Praterstern ersetzte ein zusammengewürfeltes und heruntergekommenes Ensemble durch einen einheitlichen Bau mit transparentem Dach, das den großzügigen Innenraum erhellt und den Zugang zu den Bahnsteigen vereinfacht. Die Fassade mit Einlageelementen reflektiert den Sonnenstand bzw. die Lichter der umliegenden Gebäude und lässt den von Boris Podrecca gestalteten Vorplatz einladend erscheinen. Wimmer wurde auch mit dem Neubau des Wiener Hauptbahnhofs beauftragt.

La nouvelle gare du Wien Praterstern, réalisée par Albert Wimmer, a supplanté un ensemble discordant et vétuste pour laisser place à un bâtiment homogène au toit transparent qui illumine le bel espace intérieur et facilite l'accès aux quais. Avec ses éléments encastrés, la façade reflète le soleil et aussi la lumière des bâtiments environnants éclairés pendant la nuit et met en valeur le parvis conçu par Boris Podrecca. Wimmer s'est aussi vu confier la construction de la gare centrale de Vienne.

In seguito alla ristrutturazione della stazione Wien Praterstern eseguita da Albert Wimmer, il caotico insieme di strutture fatiscenti che prima era questa stazione ferroviaria ha lasciato posto a una costruzione omogenea con tetto trasparente che illumina l'ampio interno e facilita l'accesso ai binari. La facciata con elementi di sostegno riflette il sole o, di notte, le luci degli edifici circostanti e valorizza la piazza antistante, opera di Boris Podrecca. A Wimmer è stata affidata anche la ristrutturazione della stazione principale di Vienna.

ARCHITECTURE 69

BAHNHOF WIEN PRATERSTERN

Praterstern // 2nd district, Leopoldstadt

U1, U2 Praterstern

A

UNIQA TOWER + SOFITEL VIENNA STEPHANSDOM

At night, Heinz Neumann's 250 ft. tall UNIQA Tower on the shore of the Danube Canal displays a spectacular light installation with a 75,000-sq.-ft. LED media facade that points the way to other architectural sights, such as Jean Nouvel's first project in Vienna since the Gasometer, a hotel opposite the Schwedenplatz, or Hans Hollein's Media Tower. Nearby, the beginning of Praterstraße is increasingly becoming a shopping and design destination.

Heinz Neumanns 75 m hoher UNIQA Tower am Ufer des Donaukanals zeigt des Nachts eine spektakuläre Lichtinstallation in Form einer 7 000 m² großen LED-Medienfassade, die den Weg zu weiteren architektonischen Sehenswürdigkeiten weist, wie etwa zu Jean Nouvels erstem Wienprojekt seit dem Gasometer, einem Hotel vis-à-vis des Schwedenplatzes oder Hans Holleins Media Tower. Daneben entwickelt sich auch der Beginn der anliegenden Praterstraße immer mehr zur Shopping- und Designmeile.

ARCHITECTURE 71

D'une hauteur de 75 m, l'UNIQA Tower, située au bord du canal du Danube et réalisée par Heinz Neumann, arbore une installation lumineuse spectaculaire. Sa façade multimédia de 7 000 m² composée de LEDs, s'inscrit dans la lignée d'autres curiosités architecturales comme le projet de Jean Nouvel ayant suivi le fameux gazomètre, un hôtel situé face à la Schwedenplatz, ou la Media Tower de Hans Hollein. Le début de la rue attenante, la Praterstraße est par ailleurs en passe de devenir un royaume du shopping et du design.

L'UNIQA Tower, una torre di 75 m costruita da Heinz Neumann sul Canale del Danubio, sfoggia di notte una spettacolare facciata multimediale illuminata a LED di 7 000 m² che indirizza verso altre meraviglie architettoniche della città, come per esempio l'hotel davanti a Schwedenplatz, la prima opera di Jean Nouvel realizzata a Vienna dai tempi del gasometro, o la Media Tower di Hans Hollein. L'adiacente tratto iniziale della Praterstraße si sta affermando sempre più come via dello shopping e del design.

A

UNIQA TOWER

Untere Donaustraße 21 // 2nd district, Leopoldstadt
www.uniqagroup.com

U1, U4 Schwedenplatz

ARCHITECTURE 73

SOFITEL VIENNA STEPHANSDOM

Praterstraße 1–7 // 2nd district, Leopoldstadt
Tel.: +43 (0)1 906 16-0
www.sofitel.com

U1, U4 Schwedenplatz

A

WAGNER:WERK MUSEUM POSTSPARKASSE

ARCHITECTURE 75

A

WAGNER:WERK
MUSEUM POSTSPARKASSE

Georg-Coch-Platz 2 // 1st district, Innere Stadt
Tel.: +43 (0)1 534 53 33-088
www.ottowagner.com

Mon–Fri 9 am to 5 pm, Sat 10 am to 5 pm
Tram 1, 2 Julius-Raab-Platz

ARCHITECTURE 77

Over 100 years after its completion, the main building of the Postsparkasse still reflects Otto Wagner's visionary spirit with which the famous Vienna architect revolutionized the stylistic vocabulary of his time in the early 20th century—from the steel-glass canopy of the main banking hall to the stools to the legendary aluminum exhausts of the ventilation system. Since its general renovation in 2005, the building now also houses a museum with changing exhibits, and the small banking hall is once again open to the public.

Auch mehr als 100 Jahre nach seiner Fertigstellung spiegelt das Gebäude den visionären Geist Otto Wagners wider, mit dem der Wiener Architekt Anfang des 20. Jahrhunderts die Formensprache seiner Zeit revolutionierte – vom Stahl-Glas-Baldachin des Großen Kassensaals über den Sparkassenhocker bis zu den legendären Aluminium-Auslässen der Belüftungsanlage. Seit der 2005 abgeschlossenen Sanierung beherbergt das Gebäude ein Museum mit wechselnden Ausstellungen; auch der Kleine Kassensaal ist wieder öffentlich zugänglich.

Plus de 100 ans après la fin de sa construction, le bâtiment principal de la Postsparkasse continue de refléter l'esprit visionnaire d'Otto Wagner, le célèbre architecte viennois qui a révolutionné le langage des formes au début du XIXe siècle. Le baldaquin en acier et verre de la salle des caisses et les sorties en aluminium du système d'aération en sont de parfaits exemples. Depuis la fin des travaux de rénovation en 2005, le bâtiment abrite un musée avec des expositions temporaires et la petite salle des caisses est à nouveau accessible.

Dopo oltre un secolo di vita, l'edificio principale della Postsparkasse riflette ancora lo spirito visionario del celebre architetto viennese Otto Wagner, che a inizio del XX secolo rivoluzionò l'arte visiva dell'epoca con il soffitto in vetro e acciaio della grande sala casse, lo sgabello e gli erogatori in alluminio dell'impianto d'areazione di questa banca. Dal 2005, quando è terminato un intervento di ristrutturazione generale, l'edificio ospita un museo con mostre temporanee e pure la piccola sala casse è di nuovo aperta al pubblico.

A

HAAS-HAUS

Stock-im-Eisen-Platz 4 // 1st district, Innere Stadt

U1, U3 Stephansplatz

ARCHITECTURE 79

Due in part to its privileged location across from St. Stephen's Cathedral, Hans Hollein's Haas Haus was highly controversial when it was built in 1990. The building and its curved façade are centred around the historical quadrant corner of the old Roman castrum. This architectural ensemble on Stock-im-Eisen-Platz and Stephansplatz stands as a statement of our times, yet it still fits in largely due to its mirrored glass facade.

Bedingt durch seine privilegierte Lage gegenüber dem Stephansdom, sorgte Hans Holleins Neubau des Haas-Hauses 1990 für heftige Kontroversen. Das Gebäude zentriert sich mit seiner gekurvten Fassade um das viertelkreisförmige historische Eck des alten römischen Kastrums. Es bildet im Gebäudeensemble des Stock-im-Eisen-Platzes/Stephansplatzes ein Statement unserer Zeit und bezieht dieses durch die verspiegelten Außenflächen doch mit ein

Bénéficiant d'un emplacement privilégié, en face du Stephansdom (cathédrale St-Étienne), ce bâtiment esquissé par Hans Hollein en 1990 a suscité la controverse. Le bâtiment et sa façade courbée sont centrés autour de l'angle historique, en quart de cercle, du castrum romain. Cet ensemble architectural des Stock-im-Eisen-Platz et Stephansplatz restera représentatif de notre ère, mais ses surfaces vitrées réfléchissantes lui permettent cependant de s'y intégrer.

Per la sua privilegiata ubicazione di fronte al Duomo di Santo Stefano, nel 1990 la costruzione della Haas-Haus di Hans Hollein sollevò accese polemiche. L'edificio, con la sua facciata arcuata, si sviluppa attorno alla storica sezione di forma quadrangolare dell'antico castro romano. La struttura si presenta come uno statement dell'epoca moderna tra gli edifici che popolano Stock-im-Eisen-Platz/Stephansplatz, che tuttavia riprende con le sue superfici riflettenti.

Adolf Loos' only commercial building dating from 1911 was not recognized as epochal and trendsetting until decades later due to the lack of ornamentation on its façade (nicknamed a "house without eyebrows"), particularly in contrast to the grandeur of the Hofburg located across from it. It was designated a historic building in 1947. After a complete renovation in 1987, it now houses the branch office of a bank, which is why visitors can view only parts of its complex and magnificent mahagony-studded interior.

Adolf Loos' einziger Geschäftshausbau von 1911 wurde wegen dem Verzicht auf Ornamentik an seiner Fassade („Haus ohne Augenbrauen"), der besonders zum Prunk der gegenüberliegenden Hofburg in Kontrast steht, erst Jahrzehnte später als epochales und zukunftsweisendes Bauwerk erkannt; seit 1947 steht es unter Denkmalschutz. Nach einer kompletten Renovierung 1987 beherbergt es die Filiale einer Bank, daher ist seine räumlich komplexe und prunkvolle Innengestaltung mit Mahagoni für Besucher nur teilweise zugänglich.

L'unique immeuble commercial conçu par Adolf Loos en 1911, fut à l'époque source de polémique car la sobriété de sa façade (« maison sans sourcils ») contrastait avec le fastueux Hofburg situé en face. C'est seulement plus tard qu'il fut considéré comme un édifice futuriste significatif. Il est classé monument historique depuis 1947. Depuis la restauration complète de 1987, il abrite la filiale d'une banque. Les touristes ne peuvent donc admirer qu'une partie de son architecture intérieure complexe et opulente composée de acajou.

Il valore storico e lo stile innovativo di questa struttura del 1911, l'unica ad uso commerciale realizzata da Adolf Loos, furono riconosciuti solo decenni dopo, causa la mancanza di decorazioni sulla facciata (da cui "casa senza sopracciglia") in netto contrasto con il sontuoso Hofburg situato di fronte; dal 1947 è sotto la tutela dei beni culturali. Completamente rinnovata nel 1987, oggi ospita la filiale di una banca, pertanto il suo sfarzoso interno in mogano, dalla complessa organizzazione degli spazi, è accessibile al pubblico solo in parte.

ARCHITECTURE 81

LOOSHAUS

Michaelerplatz 3 // 1st district, Innere Stadt

U3 Herrengasse

A

Integrated into Vienna's MuseumsQuartier and founded in 1993, the center for architecture Az W profits from its location in one of the most beautiful collections of Viennese Baroque buildings by Fischer von Erlach. The Az W holds exhibitions, lectures, and excursions, has a large archive, boasts a comprehensive database of (primarily Austrian) architecture, and has a public library with almost 30,000 titles. The café and restaurant Milo designed by Anne Lacaton and Jean Philippe Vassal has a striking vaulted ceiling clad with ornamental tiles.

Integriert in das Wiener MuseumsQuartier profitiert das 1993 gegründete Architekturzentrum von seiner Lage in einem der schönsten Wiener Barockensembles von Fischer von Erlach. Das Az W ist Veranstalter von Ausstellungen, Vorträgen und Exkursionen, verfügt über ein großes Archiv, eine umfassende Datenbank über (vornehmlich heimische) Architektur und eine frei zugängliche Fachbibliothek mit knapp 30 000 Titeln. Das Café und Restaurant Milo von Anne Lacaton und Jean Philippe Vassal beeindruckt durch sein Gewölbe mit Ornamentfliesen.

Intégré au MuseumsQuartier situé dans le magnifique ensemble baroque de Fischer von Erlach, le Centre d'architecture de Vienne (Az W), fondé en 1993, bénéficie d'une situation exceptionnelle. L'Az W propose des expositions, conférences et excursions, il dispose de grandes archives, d'une vaste banque de données (surtout nationale) sur l'architecture et d'une bibliothèque spécialisée libre d'accès dotée de 30 000 ouvrages. Le café restaurant Milo d'Anne Lacaton et Jean Philippe Vassal arbore une superbe voûte animée de carreaux ornementaux.

Incastonato nel MuseumsQuartier e fondato nel 1993, il Centro di Architettura di Vienna (Az W) gode della sua posizione in uno dei più affascinati isolati di edifici barocchi progettati da Fischer von Erlach. L'Az W organizza esposizioni, seminari e visite e possiede un ampio archivio di materiale storico, una vasta banca dati relativi all'architettura (specialmente austriaca) e una biblioteca specializzata aperta al pubblico con quasi 30 000 volumi. Il caffè/ristorante Milo di Anne Lacaton e Jean Philippe Vassal sfoggia un'ammirevole volta decorata con piastrelle ornamentali.

ARCHITECTURE 83

ARCHITEKTURZENTRUM WIEN

MuseumsQuartier, Museumsplatz 1 //
7th district, Neubau
Tel.: +43 (0)1 522 31 15
www.azw.at

Mon–Sun 10 am to 7 pm
U2 Museumsquartier, U2, U3 Volkstheater

PETER NOEVER

Peter Noever has been a trendsetter since the end of the 1960s through his activities as a museum expert, designer, architect, and media interventionist. As the initiator and artistic director behind the complete overhaul of the MAK, he has left his mark on the museum's distinctive identity, developed new exhibition strategies and, between tradition and experiment, has and developed new exhibition strategies. With the founding of the MAK Center for Art and Architecture in Los Angeles, and through the MAK Schindler Scholarship Program and the MAK Urban Future Initiative (UFI) as well as in cooperation with the MUAR/Shchusev State Museum of Architecture in Moscow, Noever has established MAK as an interface for global communication. Noever's vehement advocacy for a radical avant-garde movement and its autonomy as well as his fundamental critique of the system have opened new perspectives within the international contemporary museum landscape. Noever intends to use the Contemporary Art Tower (CAT) project in conjunction with the 21st century collection to realize those perspectives. The pugnacious Noever, prominent advocate of architecture and mediator between American and European positions, believes that "the quality of architecture can be found in its originality, but also in its perception of the present with all its demands and the intuition of worthwhile future developments. If for no other reason than that, the foundation of any architecture must be conflict."

Seit dem Ende der 1960er Jahre gehen vom Wirken des Museosophen, Designers, Architekten und Medieninterventionisten Peter Noever wesentliche Impulse aus. Als Initiator und künstlerischer Leiter des Generalumbaus des MAK prägte er die unverwechselbare Identität des Museums, entwickelte zwischen Tradition und Experiment neue Strategien zur Präsentation und etablierte das MAK als Schnittstelle globaler Kommunikation. Noevers vehementes Eintreten für eine radikale Avantgarde und ihre Autonomie sowie seine grundsätzliche Systemkritik haben innerhalb der zeitgenössischen internationalen Museumslandschaft neue

PORTRAIT 85

Perspektiven eröffnet, die er auch im Projekt CAT – Contemporary Art Tower mit der Sammlung des 21. Jahrhunderts verwirklichen will. Für den kämpferischen Noever, profilierter Fürsprecher der Baukunst und Mittler zwischen amerikanischen und europäischen Positionen, liegt „die Qualität der Architektur in ihrer Originalität, somit aber auch in der Wahrnehmung der Gegenwart mit allen ihren Erfordernissen und dem Erfühlen einer erstrebenswerten zukünftigen Entwicklung. Schon allein deswegen muss die Grundlage jeder Architektur der Konflikt sein."

Depuis la fin des années 1960, l'influence de Peter Noever, ce muséologue, designer, architecte et auteur engagé de plusieurs publications, ne cesse de s'accroître. En tant que fondateur et directeur artistique lors de la restauration du musée autrichien des arts appliqués (MAK), il influa sur l'identité du musée et développa de nouvelles stratégies muséales entre le traditionnel et l'expérimental et fit du MAK un point de jonction pour la communication globale entre différentes institutions internationales. Noever, à travers son engagement en vue de promouvoir une avant-garde radicale et autonome et sa tendance systématique à critiquer le système, a ouvert de nouvelles perspectives dans le monde international des musées contemporains, comme il le démontre par son projet CAT – Contemporary Art Tower avec sa collection d'œuvres du XXIe siècle. Noever, grand fervent d'architecture et médiateur entre les courants américains et européens, considère que « la qualité de l'architecture réside dans son originalité, mais également dans la perception du présent et la reconnaissance des évolutions futures. C'est pourquoi le fondement de chaque architecture doit être le conflit ».

Con il suo operato, il patrocinatore delle arti, designer, architetto e commentatore mediatico Peter Noever mantiene i riflettori puntati su di sé sin dalla fine degli anni '60. Quale promotore e direttore artistico dell'ambizioso progetto di rilancio del MAK, Noever è l'artefice dell'inconfondibile personalità del museo e di nuove strategie di presentazione artistica al confine fra tradizione e sperimentazione e ha fatto emergere il MAK come interfaccia della comunicazione globale. L'impeto con cui Noevers si batte per un profondo atteggiamento avanguardistico nell'arte e per l'autonomia di quest'ultima, così come la sua netta opposizione ai sistemi organizzativi, hanno aperto nuove prospettive sul panorama artistico internazionale della nostra epoca, prospettive che l'artista vuole realizzare anche nell'ambito del progetto CAT – Contemporary Art Tower con la creazione in situ di una collezione del XXI secolo. Per il combattivo Noever, autorevole sostenitore dell'arte architettonica e mediatore tra posizioni americane ed europee, "la qualità dell'architettura sta nella sua originalità, ma allo stesso tempo anche nella percezione del presente con tutte le sue esigenze e nell'intuizione di un auspicabile sviluppo nel futuro. Anche solo in virtù di ciò, alla base di ogni opera architettonica deve stare il conflitto".

A

GÜRTEL

Otto Wagner's viaduct now houses trendy stores, boosting values tremendously. This transformation has inspired others nearby, for instance Ernst Mayr's 2003 design of the Hauptbücherei (main city library), a striking ship-like building with Vienna's largest flight of stairs located across from Roland Rainer's 1958-era Stadthalle (city hall); the IP-TWO Center (BKK-3, 2003); and the Skywalk, a footbridge connecting the once separated neighborhoods. To best appreciate Silja Tillner's revitalization concept, join a tour offered by the Az W.

Otto Wagners Stadtbahnbögen erfuhren durch die Integration von Szenelokalen eine massive Aufwertung. Auch die anliegende Architektur wurde dadurch beflügelt, so Ernst Mayrs seit 2003 gegenüber Roland Rainers Stadthalle von 1958 liegende Hauptbücherei in Form eines Schiffs mit Wiens größter Freitreppe, das IP-TWO Center (von BKK-3, 2003) oder der Skywalk, eine Brücke, die die einst getrennten Stadtteile nun verbindet. Silja Tillners Revitalisierungskonzept erschließt sich am besten bei einer vom Architekturzentrum Wien veranstalteten Tour.

ARCHITECTURE 87

Les arcades de métro d'Otto Wagner ont été fortement valorisées par l'installation de nombreux établissements. L'architecture environnante a elle aussi été dynamisée, citons par ex. l'Hauptbücherei (bibliothèque principale) en forme de bateau d'Ernst Mayrs (2003), qui se situe en face de la Stadthalle (salle polyvalente) de Roland Rainer (1958), le centre IP-TWO de BBK-3, (2003) ou le Skywalk, un pont reliant les parties de la ville autrefois séparées. Pour admirer le concept de redynamisation de Silja Tillner, le mieux est de participer à la visite organisée par l'Az W.

Le stazioni della metropolitana di Otto Wagner sono state valorizzate dalla nascita di ambienti "in" di cui hanno beneficiato anche gli edifici vicini, come la Hauptbücherei (biblioteca centrale), realizzata nel 2003 da Ernst Mayr di fronte alla Stadthalle di Roland Rainer (1958) a guisa di nave e con la scalinata esterna più grande di Vienna, l'IP-TWO Center di BKK-3, (2003) e lo Skywalk, un ponte che unisce le parti della città un tempo divise. Tale progetto di rilancio concepito da Silja Tillner è ben illustrato dai tour organizzati dall'Az W.

IP-TWO

Lerchenfelder Gürtel 43 //
16th district, Ottakring

U6 Josefstädter Straße

Informationen on Az W Tour 9
"Der Gürtel": Architekturzentrum Wien
Tel.: +43 (0)1 522 31 15-11, www.azw.at

WIENER STADTHALLE

Vogelweidplatz 14 //
15th district,
Rudolfsheim-Fünfhaus
www.stadthalle.com

U6 Burggasse/Stadthalle

ARCHITECTURE 89

HAUPTBÜCHEREI WIEN

Urban-Loritz-Platz 2a //
7th district, Neubau
www.buechereien.wien.at

U6 Burggasse/Stadthalle

SKYWALK + SKYLINE

Heiligenstädter Straße 29–31 //
19th district, Döbling

U4/U6 Spittelau

HAUS RAY1

Mittersteig 10 // 5th district, Margareten

Bus 13A Leibenfrostgasse

ARCHITECTURE 91

Designed by Vienna architects Delugan Meissl Associated Architects and finished in 2003, Haus Ray1 is an impressive extension added on to the flat roof of a 1960s era office building. The aluminum facade visible from the street is transected by long bands of windows, and the geometry of horizontal, vertical and diagonal levels is continued in the interior of the loft. The use of load-bearing glass provides for spectacular views of Vienna.

Das 2003 fertiggestellte Haus Ray1 von Delugan Meissl Associated Architects sitzt als eindrucksvolle Dachaufstockung auf einem Bürogebäude aus den 1960er Jahren. Die von der Straße aus sichtbare Aluminiumfassade wird von langgezogenen Fensterbändern durchschnitten, die Geometrie aus horizontalen, vertikalen und diagonalen Ebenen setzt sich im Inneren des Lofts fort, der Einsatz von tragendem Glas erlaubt spektakuläre Ausblicke auf Wien.

La Haus Ray1, réalisée par viennois Delugan Meissl Associated Architects et terminée en 2003, est une impressionnante surélévation de toit juchée sur un immeuble de bureaux des années 1960. La façade en aluminium visible depuis la rue est divisée par de longues bandes de fenêtres, la géométrie composée de plans horizontaux, verticaux et diagonaux se poursuit à l'intérieur du loft. Enfin, l'utilisation de verre porteur offre une vue spectaculaire sur la ville.

Ultimata nel 2003 su progetto dello studio di viennese Delugan Meissl Associated Architects, la Haus Ray1 si presenta come notevole sopraedificazione di un edificio adibito a uffici degli anni '60. La facciata di alluminio, visibile dalla strada, è tagliata da una lunga serie di finestre poste l'una accanto all'altra, la geometria di piani orizzontali, verticali e diagonali prosegue anche all'interno del loft e l'utilizzo di vetro portante consente di ammirare vedute spettacolari della città.

A

GASOMETER

ARCHITECTURE 93

A

Vienna's most spectacular construction project in decades is the transformation of what was one of the largest gas works in Europe (1896–99) into apartments, student housing, offices, restaurants, cinemas, casinos, etc. Each tank was assigned to a famous architectural team (Gasometer A: Jean Nouvel; B: Coop Himmelb(l)au; C: Wehdorn Architekten; D: Wilhelm Holzbauer). Although it has not yet revitalized the surrounding area as hoped, it is still an impressive example of how former industrial sites can be transformed.

Wiens spektakulärstes Bauprojekt der letzten Jahrzehnte bestand in der Verwandlung der vier Zylinder des einst größten Gaswerks Europas (1896–99) in Wohnungen, Studentenheim, Geschäfte, Restaurants, Kino, Kasino, etc. Jeder Speicher hat ein renommiertes Architektenbüro gestaltet (Gasometer A: Jean Nouvel, B: Coop Himmelb(l)au, C: Wehdorn Architekten, D: Wilhelm Holzbauer). Wiewohl die Hoffnung, damit auch die Umgebung neu zu beleben, bisher unerfüllt blieb, ist es ein beeindruckendes Beispiel für die Umwandlung von Industriemonumenten.

Le projet de construction le plus spectaculaire des dernières décennies a été la transformation des quatre cylindres de cette ancienne usine à gaz (1896–99) en logements, commerces, restaurants, etc. La réalisation des réservoirs a été confiée à des bureaux d'architectes renommés : Gazomètre A : Jean Nouvel, B : Coop Himmelb(l)au, C : Wehdorn Architekten, D : Wilhelm Holzbauer). Bien que ce projet n'ait jusqu'à présent pas réussi à dynamiser le quartier comme escompté, il reste un exemple exceptionnel de reconversion de bâtiments industriels.

Il più grandioso progetto urbanistico di Vienna degli ultimi decenni è stata la conversione della ex centrale del gas più grande d'Europa (1896–99) in appartamenti, case dello studente, negozi, ristoswqmato studio d'architettura (gasometro A: Jean Nouvel, B: Coop Himmelb(l)au, C: Wehdorn Architekten, D: Wilhelm Holzbauer). Benché non si sia riusciti a rivitalizzare anche l'area circostante, il complesso è un notevole esempio di trasformazione di mastodonti industriali.

ARCHITECTURE 95

GASOMETER

Guglgasse 6 // 11th district, Simmering
www.wiener-gasometer.at

U3 Gasometer

A

T-CENTER ST. MARX

ARCHITECTURE 97

A

Until it was finished in 2004, this 33-acre office and business center designed by the architectural team of Domenig/Eisenköck/Peyker was Austria's largest private development. The reclining skyscraper sculpture with a towering wing is traversed by walkways, and due to its striking integration into the structural context was awarded the Otto Wagner Urban Development Prize in 2004.

Bis zu seiner Fertigstellung 2004 war dieses vom Architektenteam Domenig/Eisenköck/Peyker entworfene Büro- und Geschäftsgebäude mit 134 000 m² Österreichs größtes privates Bauvorhaben. Die liegende Hochhausskulptur mit emporragendem Flügel ist von Wegen durchzogen und wurde wegen ihrer markanten Einbindung in den baulichen Kontext mit dem Otto Wagner Städtebaupreis 2004 ausgezeichnet.

Jusqu'à la fin de sa construction en 2004, ce projet d'immeuble commercial et de bureaux d'une surface de 134 000 m², conçu par l'équipe d'architectes Domenig/Eisenköck/Peyker était le plus grand projet de construction privée en Autriche. La structure horizontale de cet immeuble au flanc orienté vers le ciel et traversée par des passages s'est vue récompenser du prix Otto Wagner pour la planification urbaine pour son intégration remarquée dans l'environnement architectural.

Fino al momento della sua realizzazione, avvenuta nel 2004, questo centro di 134 000 m² con uffici e negozi ideato dallo studio di architettura Domenig/Eisenköck/Peyker è stato il progetto di costruzione di un edificio privato più grande d'Austria. Si tratta di una sorta di immensa scultura a forma digrattacielo disteso con un'inconfondibile ala svettante attraversata da vari collegamenti che nel 2004 ha ottenuto il premio di urbanistica Otto Wagner per il suo rimarchevole inserimento nel contesto edilizio.

ARCHITECTURE 99

T-CENTER ST. MARX

Rennweg 97–99 // 3rd district, Landstraße

S7 St. Marx, Bus 74A St. Marx,
Tram 18, 71 St. Marx

A

WIENERBERG CITY

ARCHITECTURE 101

A

WIENERBERG CITY

Between Wienerbergstraße, Clemens-Holzmeister-Straße,
Hertha-Firnberg-Straße, and Rotdornallee // 10th district, Favoriten

Bus 15A, 65A, 7B Business Park Vienna

ARCHITECTURE 103

1999 marked the year that construction began on Wienerberg City, a group of residential and commercial high-rise buildings surrounding a newly designed lake and park in the Favoriten district. In 2001 the Vienna Twin Towers by Massimiliano Fuksas were the first buildings to be completed. The complex also includes the City Lofts designed by Delugan Meissl Associated Architects, business apartments by Cuno Brullmann, and the Monte Verde apartment tower by Albert Wimmer with its green glass and ceramic facade and Vienna's highest swimming pool.

1999 wurde in Wien-Favoriten mit dem Bau der Wienerberg City begonnen, eine Anordnung zahlreicher Wohn- und Bürohochhäuser rund um einen neu gestalteten See und Park. 2001 wurden als erste Gebäude die Vienna Twin Towers von Massimiliano Fuksas fertiggestellt. Das Areal umfasst unter anderem die City Lofts von Delugan Meissl Associated Architects, Businessapartments von Cuno Brullmann und den Monte-Verde-Wohnturm von Albert Wimmer mit seiner grünen Glas-Keramik-Fassade und Wiens höchstgelegenem Schwimmbad.

En 1999, la construction du Wienerberg City, des immeubles d'habitation et de bureaux autour d'un lac et d'un parc nouvellement aménagés, a été lancée dans l'arrondissement Favoriten. Les Vienna Twin Towers de Massimiliano Fuksas ont été les premières à sortir de terre en 2001. Ce pôle englobe entre autres les City Lofts de Delugan Meissl Associated Architects, des appartements d'affaires de Cuno Brullmann et la tour d'habitation Monte Verde d'Albert Wimmer avec sa façade en verre et céramique et la piscine de Vienne la plus haute en altitude.

Nel 1999 iniziò a Favoriten la costruzione di Wienerberg City, un fitto insieme di edifici residenziali e per uffici raccolto intorno a una nuova zona provvista di lago e parco. Le prime costruzioni ultimate furono, nel 2001, le Vienna Twin Tower di Massimiliano Fuksas. L'area comprende inoltre i City Loft del Delugan Meissl Associated Architects, gli appartamenti commerciali di Cuno Brullmann e Monte Verde, una torre residenziale di Albert Wimmer con facciata in ceramica e vetro verde e la piscina in posizione più alta di tutta Vienna.

A

When the cable factory closed in 1997, the Kabelwerk became an urban development project. After housing a variety of cultural projects, it became the latest large-scale residential building project. Construction began in 2004 under the guidance of several architectural teams; since 2005, the buildings have been gradually turned over to residents. This diverse yet harmonious complex includes apartments, businesses, geriatrics center, preschools, and recreational areas (panorama swimming pool), interspersed with paths, courtyards, green areas, and playgrounds.

Nach seiner Schließung 1997 wurde das Kabelwerk zum Stadtentwicklungsprojekt. Als jüngster großer Wohnbau wurde 2004 nach einer Nutzung für kulturelle Projekte unter der Leitung mehrerer Architektenteams die Bebauung aufgenommen; die Bauten werden seit 2005 sukzessive an die Bewohner übergeben. Das divergente, aber harmonische Areal umfasst Wohnungen, Geschäfte, Geriatriezentrum, Kindergärten und Freizeiteinrichtungen (Panoramaschwimmbad), dazwischen befinden sich Promenaden, Plätze, Grün- und Spielflächen.

Fermé en 1997, le Kabelwerk (usine de câbles) a fait l'objet d'un projet de développement de la ville. Après avoir servi à divers projets culturels, il a bénéficié d'un grand projet de construction d'immeubles d'habitation, débuté par plusieurs équipes d'architectes en 2004. Les logements sont livrés les uns après les autres depuis 2005. Le pôle hétérogène mais harmonieux englobe des logements, commerces, centre de gériatrie, crèches et lieux de loisirs (piscine panoramique) mais aussi des promenades, places, espaces verts et espaces de jeux.

Dalla sua chiusura, nel 1997, questa ex fabbrica di cavi è diventata un progetto di sviluppo urbanistico. Dopo un periodo di utilizzo per scopi culturali, nel 2004 iniziò il più grande progetto urbanistico d'ultima generazione sotto la guida di varie equipe di architetti; dal 2005 le costruzioni vengono gradualmente destinate a uso residenziale. Questo complesso vario e al contempo armonico comprende appartamenti, negozi, centro di geriatria, asili e strutture per il tempo libero (piscina panoramica), intercalati da viali, piazze, aree verdi e parchi giochi.

ARCHITECTURE 105

KABELWERK

Oswaldgasse 33 // 12th district, Meidling
www.kabelwerk.at

U6 Tscherttegasse

DESIGN

D

Design has tradition in this former capital of the monarchy, and as Josef Hoffmann, Otto Wagner or Koloman Moser did in their day, today you can witness young and often internationally successful creative personalities who, with their designs, objects and shops, create a current and exciting scene. Visitors can choose from an array of possibilities: from exhibitions, lectures, symposiums, and Vienna Design Week—Austria's largest fashion festival—to fashion stores with architectural interest, hotels whose contemporary interiors contrast with their historical exteriors, to the new restaurant scene. One classic hot spot with a notable interior architecture is the Loosbar: Adolf Loos was a pioneer of modern design in Vienna and designed this small American Bar over 100 years ago. Today, well-known architects such as Sir Terence Conran, Hermann Czech and Eichinger oder Knechtl continue the tradition of creating bars and restaurants which are well worth experiencing if for no other reason than for their design.

Design hat Tradition in der ehemaligen Hauptstadt der Monarchie, und so wie damals Josef Hoffmann, Otto Wagner oder Koloman Moser sind es heute junge, auch international erfolgreiche Kreativschaffende, die mit ihren Entwürfen, Objekten und Shops für die aktuelle, spannende Szene stehen. Das Angebot reicht von Ausstellungen, Vorträgen, Symposien und der Vienna Design Week, Österreichs größtem Festival in diesem Bereich, über Fashionstores mit Architekturerlebnis und Hotels, deren zeitgenössisches Interieur in Kontrast zur historischen Bausubstanz steht, bis zur neuen Gastroszene. Klassiker der Lokale mit besonderer Innenarchitektur ist wohl die Loosbar des Pioniers der Moderne aus Wien, der diese kleine American Bar vor 100 Jahren entworfen hat. Auch heute sind es namhafte Architekten, wie Sir Terence Conran, Hermann Czech, Eichinger oder Knechtl, die Lokale geschaffen haben, die schon wegen ihres Designs erlebenswert sind.

INTRO DESIGN   109

L'ancienne capitale de la monarchie possède également sa tradition du design. Tout comme ce fut le cas à l'époque avec Josef Hoffmann, Otto Wagner ou Koloman Moser, des jeunes artistes de renommée internationale sont, à travers leurs esquisses, objets et boutiques, le reflet de cette nouvelle génération artistique. Pour admirer ce nouveau style, l'offre est infinie : des expositions, conférences, symposiums et de la Vienna Design Week, le plus grand festival du design d'Autriche, en passant par les boutiques de mode à l'architecture design et les hôtels dont l'aménagement contemporain contraste avec le style des bâtiments historiques, jusqu'aux établissements gastronomiques. Comme grand classique, nous évoquerons ici le bar américain Loosbar, établissement au décor intérieur particulier, qui fut imaginé il y a 100 ans par l'un des pionniers du modernisme viennois, Adolf Loos. Mais n'oublions pas d'illustres architectes comme Sir Terence Conran, Hermann Czech, Eichinger ou Knechtl dont les établissements présentent un intérieur design qui vaut le détour.

Il design ha alle spalle una lunga tradizione nella ex capitale imperiale, e come allora fecero Josef Hoffmann, Otto Wagner o Koloman Moser, adesso sono giovani e affermati artisti internazionali dall'estro creativo, con i loro progetti, le loro creazioni e i negozi, e rendere così stuzzicante il settore del design nella Vienna di oggi. La gamma di offerte in questo campo comprende mostre, seminari, simposi e la Vienna Design Week, il più grande festival del design d'Austria, passando per negozi di moda ospitati in edifici dal notevole design architettonico e alberghi con un interno in stile moderno in forte contrasto con il modello edilizio della struttura che li ospita, fino ad arrivare al nuovo panorama gastronomico. Esempio emblematico di locali con una particolare architettura degli interni è il Loosbar, opera del pioniere del Modernismo viennese che progettò questo bar in stile americano un secolo fa. Ancora oggi sono celebri architetti come Sir Terence Conran, Hermann Czech, Eichinger o Knechtl gli artefici di locali che merita visitare anche solo per ammirare il loro design.

D

HOLLMANN BELETAGE

Köllnerhofgasse 6 // 1st district, Innere Stadt
Tel.: +43 (0)1 961 19 60
www.hollmann-beletage.at

U1, U3 Stephansplatz, U1, U4 Schwedenplatz

Located not far from the Stephansplatz, the Hollmann Beletage is Vienna's smallest design and boutique hotel. Owner Robert Hollmann commissioned architect Christian Prasser to design 25 rooms on the second and third floors of a noble Wilhelminian style building. The bright, spacious rooms are furnished with warm, dark wood; a functional partition wall creates space, as does a freestanding bathtub open to the room. The hotel has a central living room with fireplace, library and piano that is open to all guests.

Unweit des Stephansplatzes liegt die Hollmann Beletage, Wiens kleinstes Design- und Boutiquehotel. Auf der ersten und zweiten Etage eines noblen Gründerzeithauses ließ Besitzer Robert Hollmann 25 Zimmer von Architekt Christian Prasser gestalten. Die hellen, großzügigen Räume sind mit warmem, dunklem Holz möbliert, eine funktionelle Einbauwand schafft viel Platz, ebenso wie das offene Wohnbad mit freistehender Wanne. Ein zentrales Wohnzimmer mit Kamin, Bibliothek und Klavier steht allen Gästen zur Verfügung.

Non loin de la Stephansplatz, dans une noble maison Gründerzeit, se trouve le plus petit hôtel-boutique design de Vienne. Robert Hollmann, le propriétaire, a confié la conception de 25 chambres du premier et du second étage à l'architecte Christian Prasser. Les grandes pièces lumineuses sont meublées de bois foncé et une étagère encastrée fonctionnelle permet une économie d'espace, tout comme la salle de bain ouverte avec baignoire îlot. Un salon central avec cheminée, bibliothèque et piano est mis à la disposition de tous les clients.

Vicino a Stephansplatz sorge l'Hollmann Beletage, il boutique hotel più piccolo di Vienna. L'albergo occupa il primo e il secondo piano di un nobile edificio in Gründerzeit e offre 25 camere disegnate dall'architetto Christian Prasser su commissione del proprietario Robert Hollmann. Le stanze, ampie e luminose, hanno caldi arredi in legno scuro, un'intelligente libreria a vista offre molto spazio, così come il bagno aperto con vasca indipendente. A disposizione di tutti gli ospiti c'è un salotto centrale con caminetto, biblioteca e pianoforte.

D

THE RING – VIENNA'S CASUAL LUXURY HOTEL

DESIGN // HOTELS   113

D

Located in a prime spot close to the Vienna State Opera, The Ring Hotel combines the traditional with the contemporary: The historic facade conceals 68 rooms and suites with modern interiors. The day spa area on the eight floor offers the best view of downtown. On the ground floor, the domed restaurant at eight tempts patrons with aroma cuisine—delicious dishes prepared with herbs and ethereal oils. The bar, Drings, offers up changing art installations.

In bester Lage, nahe der Wiener Staatsoper, vereint das The Ring Hotel Vienna Traditionelles mit Neuem: Hinter der historischen Fassade verbergen sich 68 Zimmer und Suiten mit geradlinig modern designtem Interieur. Den besten Blick über die Innenstadt bietet der Spa-Bereich auf der siebten Etage. Im Erdgeschoss lockt das haubengekrönte Restaurant at eight mit Gerichten aus der Aromaküche, die mit Kräutern und ätherischen Ölen zubereitet werden, und die Bar Drings überrascht mit wechselnden Kunstinstallationen.

The Ring Hotel, situé à proximité de l'Opéra national de Vienne, allie tradition et modernité. Derrière la superbe façade historique, cet hôtel dévoile 68 chambres et suites au design moderne. L'espace spa du septième étage offre la plus belle vue sur le centre ville. Au rez-de-chaussée, le prestigieux restaurant at eight éveille les papilles avec ses mets issus de la cuisine aromatique préparés avec herbes et huiles essentielles. Le bar Drings arbore des installations artistiques temporaires surprenantes.

Situato vicino alla Staatsoper viennese, il The Ring Hotel è un incontro di tradizione e modernità: dietro la sua storica facciata ospita infatti 68 camere e suite che sfoggiano un interno dal design lineare tipico dello stile moderno. Al settimo piano si trova un'area benessere che offre la più bella vista che si possa godere del centro. Al pianoterra, il prestigioso ristorante at eight seduce con piatti di cucina aromatica preparati con spezie e oli essenziali, e il bar Drings sorprende con installazioni artistiche sempre diverse.

DESIGN // HOTELS 115

**THE RING
VIENNA'S CASUAL LUXURY HOTEL**

Kärntner Ring 8 // 1st district, Innere Stadt
Tel.: +43 (0)1 221 22

www.theringhotel.com
U1, U2, U4 Karlsplatz/Oper

D

DAS TRIEST

DESIGN // HOTELS 117

The name of this hotel is the only reminder of its history as a stagecoach stop on the line between Vienna and Trieste. Today, Das Triest is a prime example of how a historical building can be combined with contemporary design. It's not surprising given that the hotel was designed by Sir Terence Conran. The 72 rooms and suites are decorated with custom furniture, artwork and accessories. One of the most beautiful areas in the hotel is the landscaped inner courtyard, while Silver Bar is a favorite with the style-conscious Viennese public.

An die Vergangenheit als Postkutschenstation der Verbindung Wien–Triest erinnert nur noch der Name: Das Triest präsentiert sich heute als Musterbeispiel für eine gelungene Symbiose von historischer Bausubstanz und zeitgemäßem Design. Kein Wunder, denn das Hotel wurde von Sir Terence Conran gestaltet und die 72 Zimmer und Suiten mit speziell entworfenen Möbeln, Kunstwerken und Accessoires bereichert. Zu den schönsten Plätzen zählen der begrünte Innenhof sowie die auch bei stilbewussten Wienern beliebte Silver Bar.

Seul son nom rappelle que par le passé, cet endroit fut un relais des postes aux chevaux de la ligne Vienne – Triest car aujourd'hui, cet hôtel est un modèle de symbiose réussie entre un bâtiment historique et un design contemporain. C'est Sir Terence Conran qui a aménagé l'hôtel et a décoré ses 72 chambres et suites avec des meubles uniques, des œuvres d'art et des accessoires. La superbe cour intérieure verdoyante et le Silver Bar, particulièrement affectionné des Viennois au goût prononcé pour le style, valent le détour.

Al suo passato di luogo di sosta per diligenze postali in viaggio sul tratto Vienna – Trieste allude ormai soltanto il nome: oggi Das Triest si presenta piuttosto come emblema di una perfetta simbiosi tra struttura edilizia classica e design moderno. E non c'è da stupirsi, dal momento che l'hotel è stato progettato da Sir Terence Conran e dotato di 72 camere e suite che sfoggiano mobili, opere d'arte e accessori appositamente disegnati. Magnifici il verdeggiante cortile interno e il Silver Bar, molto apprezzato dai Viennesi che amano il buon gusto.

DESIGN // HOTELS 119

DAS TRIEST

Wiedner Hauptstraße 12 // 4th district, Wieden
Tel.: +43 (0)1 589 18-0
www.dastriest.at

U1, U2, U4 Karlsplatz/Oper

D

SKOPIK & LOHN

Leopoldsgasse 17 // 2nd district, Leopoldstadt
Tel.: +43 (0)1 219 89 77
www.skopikundlohn.at

Mon–Sat and public holidays 6 pm to 1 am
U2 Taborstraße

DESIGN // RESTAURANTS

The blocks around the Karmelitermarkt have become a trendy area in recent years. Skopik & Lohn is one of the spots that is well worth a visit in this corner of the Leopoldstadt. Both visually and in terms of cuisine, it is a highly successful mixture of an upscale Viennese restaurant and a French bistro. The Wienerschnitzel and steak fries taste even better when dining under the wild ceiling painting by Austrian artist Otto Zitko, and the dessert selection in particular leaves nothing to be desired. Reservations are recommended.

Die Gegend rund um den Karmelitermarkt hat sich in den letzten Jahren zum Trendbezirk entwickelt. Zu den empfehlenswerten Plätzen in diesem Winkel der Leopoldstadt zählt das Skopik & Lohn, eine optisch wie kulinarisch gelungene Mischung aus gehobenem Wiener Restaurant und französischem Bistro. Unter dem wilden Deckengemälde des österreichischen Künstlers Otto Zitko schmecken Wiener Schnitzel und Steak Frites noch einmal so gut, und vor allem die Dessertauswahl lässt keinen Wunsch offen. Tischreservierung ist angeraten.

Le quartier situé autour du Karmelitermarkt est devenu en quelques années un quartier à la mode. Cet angle de la Leopoldstadt regorge d'endroits qui valent le détour, comme Skopik & Lohn, dont la superbe optique et la savoureuse cuisine se situent entre le restaurant viennoise raffinée et le bistrot français. Sous la fresque de plafond de l'artiste autrichien Otto Zitko, on savoure des Wiener Schnitzel, des steak frites et la carte des desserts est tout simplement fabuleuse. Réservation conseillée.

Negli ultimi anni la zona del Karmelitermarkt è diventata un quartiere di tendenza. Tra i locali degni di nota situati in questo angolo di Leopoldstadt figura lo Skopik & Lohn, fortunato intreccio ottico e gastronomico tra un ristorante viennese e un bistrò francese. Sotto un soffitto abbellito da stravaganti dipinti dell'artista Otto Zitko si riscopre il sapore di piatti tradizionali come Wiener Schnitzel e bistecca con patatine, ma sono soprattutto i dessert a non lasciare inesaudito nessun desiderio. Si consiglia di prenotare.

D

MOTTO WORLD

With his personality, Bernd Schlacher successfully used Motto, a small trendy hot spot where fashion star Helmut Lang once worked at the bar, as a springboard to develop a series of locations that draw creative personalities, artists and gourmets alike. The latest is Motto am Fluss, located at the ship terminal Wien City along the Danube Canal; it boasts a gastronomy area designed by BEHF architects that includes a restaurant, lounge, bar, and café on two different levels along with the Mottoshop, a high-end grocery store.

Bernd Schlacher gelang es mit seiner Persönlichkeit aus dem kleinen Szenelokal Motto, in dem der heutige Modestar Helmut Lang einst an der Bar arbeitete, eine ganze Reihe von Locations zu entwickeln, die Kreative, Künstler und Gourmets gleichermaßen anzieht. Neuester Standort ist das Motto am Fluss in der Schiffsstation Wien City am Donaukanal, mit einem von den Wiener BEHF Architekten gestalteten Gastronomiebereich mit Restaurant, Lounge, Bar und Café auf zwei Etagen sowie dem Mottoshop, einem Edelkrämer.

DESIGN // RESTAURANTS 123

Bernd Schlacher, créateur du petit bar Motto où la star de la mode Helmut Lang a travaillé en tant que barman, est parvenu grâce à sa personnalité à développer toute une série d'établissements qui attirent à la fois les artistes et les gourmets. Son tout dernier local, conçu par le cabinet d'architectes viennois BEHF, et qui se situe au bord du canal du Danube dans le terminal Wien City, arbore un espace gastronomique sur deux étages avec restaurant, lounge, bar, café et l'épicerie Mottoshop.

Partendo dal piccolo bar di tendenza Motto, dietro al cui bancone una volta lavorava Helmut Lang, oggi famoso stilista, con il suo tocco personale Bernd Schlacher ha creato una serie di ambienti che attraggono tanto persone dall'estro creativo quanto artisti e buongustai. Il locale di più recente apertura è situato presso il terminal della Wien City lungo il canale del Danubio, e ospita un'area ristorazione concepita dallo studio viennese BEHF e comprendente ristorante, lounge, bar e caffè disposti su due piani, nonché il raffinato Mottoshop.

MOTTO

Schönbrunner Straße 30,
Entrance Rüdigergasse //
5th district, Margareten
Tel.: +43 (0)1 587 06 72
www.motto.at/motto

Mon–Sun 6 pm to 2 am, Fri-Sat to 4 am
U4 Pilgramgasse

MOTTO AM FLUSS

Franz-Josefs-Kai between
Marienbrücke and Schwedenbrücke /
1st district, Innere Stadt
Tel.: +43 (0)1 252 55-10
(restaurant), -11 (café), -12 (shop)
www.mottoamfluss.at
Mon–Sun 11 am to 3 pm, 6 pm to 2 am
U1, U4 Schwedenplatz

DESIGN // RESTAURANTS 125

HALLE
CAFÉ-RESTAURANT

MuseumsQuartier, Museumsplatz 1 //
7th district, Neubau
Tel.: +43 (0)1 523 70 01
www.diehalle.at

Mon–Sun 10 am to 2 am
U2 Museumsquartier, U2/U3 Volkstheater

KUNSTHALLENCAFE
AM KARLSPLATZ

Treitlstraße 2 // 4th district, Wieden
Tel.: +43 (0)1 587 00 73
www.kunsthallencafe.at

Mon–Sun 10 am to 2 am
U1, U2, U4 Karlsplatz/Oper

BERND SCHLAC

Bernd Schlacher is one of the most creative hosts in this city. He began his professional career more than 25 years ago at Restaurant Wiener. Beginning in 1991 with a sure instinct of what to do, he took a small space named Motto, a local secret in the 5th district of Vienna, and created an unforgettable hot spot that adeptly combines its original flair with global ambience. Culinary quality and innovation combined with a steady hand when it comes to style and taste form the foundation for Schlacher's successful expansion. Even back in the 1990s Schlacher was one of the main movers and shakers behind the scenes of large events in Vienna. A few of Schlacher's milestones include the "Passion" clubbing events at the Vienna Technical Museum (1993) and "Starnight" at the Wiener Sophiensäle (1995/1996), which he organized together with Andy Lackner and Hannes Jagerhofer. After the successes of his restaurants in the MuseumsQuartier and at the Kunsthalle, it is not surprising that he was invited to expand his Motto world: Located at the new Twin City Liners ship terminal along the Danube Canal, Schlacher opened Motto am Fluss, his latest culinary project, in the summer of 2010.

Bernd Schlacher ist einer der kreativsten Gastgeber dieser Stadt. Im Restaurant Wiener begann vor rund 25 Jahren seine berufliche Laufbahn. Mit viel Fingerspitzengefühl hat er dann seit 1991 aus dem kleinen Geheimtipp Motto im fünften Wiener Gemeindebezirk ein unvergleichliches Szenelokal erstehen lassen, das das ursprüngliche Flair geschickt mit globalem Ambiente verbindet. Die ganz besondere Mischung aus gastronomischer Qualität und Innovation, aber auch die sichere Hand für alles, was mit Stil und Geschmack zu tun hat, sind die Säulen seiner erfolgreichen Expansion. Schon in den 1990er Jahren war Schlacher aber auch immer wieder einer der wesentlichen Drahtzieher hinter großen Events in Wien. Meilensteine waren die Clubbings „Passion" im Technischen Museum (1993) und „Starnight" in den Wiener Sophiensälen (1995/1996), die er gemeinsam mit Andy Lackner und Hannes Jagerhofer organisierte. Nach den Erfolgen seiner nächsten Lokale im Museumsquartier und in der Kunsthalle war es nicht verwunderlich, dass er eingeladen wurde, die Motto-Welt zu erweitern: In der neuen Schiffsanlegestelle des Twin City Liners am Donaukanal schuf Schlacher im Sommer 2010 mit Motto am Fluss sein neuestes gastronomisches Projekt.

PORTRAIT 127

Bernd Schlacher est l'un des hôtes les plus créatifs de la ville. Sa carrière débuta il y a 25 ans dans le restaurant Wiener. En 1991, il inaugura l'incomparable petit restaurant Motto dans le 5ᵉ arrondissement de Vienne en y combinant, avec beaucoup de doigté, le flair de l'époque à une ambiance universelle. Son succès s'appuie sur la combinaison particulière d'une gastronomie de qualité et d'un concept innovant, mais également sur son savoir-faire en ce qui concerne le style et le bon goût. Schlacher fut, déjà dans les années 1990, l'instigateur de plusieurs grands événements, comme les soirées clubbing « Passion » au Musée technique de Vienne (1993) et « Starnight » dans la salle de bal Sophiensäle (1995/1996), qu'il organisa avec Andy Lackner et Hannes Jagerhofer. Après le succès de ses différents établissements, il n'est donc pas étonnant qu'il fut invité à élargir son concept Motto. Au début de l'été 2010, il créa son nouveau concept gastronomique Motto am Fluss dans le nouvel embarcadère du Twin City Liners au bord du canal du Danube.

Bernd Schlacher è uno dei gestori di locali più creativi della città. La sua carriera ebbe inizio circa 25 anni fa nel Restaurant Wiener. Poi, partendo nel 1991 dal piccolo Motto, un gioiellino nascosto nel quinto distretto di Vienna, con grande maestria Bernd Schlacher è riuscito a creare una serie di ambienti senza uguali che combinano alla perfezione il loro fascino originario con un'atmosfera di respiro internazionale. Il particolarissimo connubio tra cucina d'alta qualità e innovazione e l'incontestabile esperienza che Schlacher dimostra in tutto ciò che ha a che fare con stile e buon gusto, sono le colonne portanti del suo ampio impero. Già negli anni '90, tuttavia, Schlacher era stato più volte uno dei principali organizzatori dietro le quinte di grandi eventi della capitale. Pietre miliari furono in tal senso la festa "Passion" organizzata nella cornice del Technisches Museum (1993) e la "Starnight" presso le Wiener Sophiensäle (1995/1996), che Bernd Schlacher orchestrò in collaborazione con Andy Lackner e Hannes Jagerhofer. Considerati i successi che poi riscossero i suoi locali nel MuseumsQuartier e nella Kunsthalle, non c'è da stupirsi se questo grande artista del design fu poi invitato ad ampliare l'universo del Motto. Così, nell'estate del 2010, presso il nuovo ormeggio della Twin City Liners sul Canale del Danubio è stato inaugurato l'ultimo paradiso gastronomico firmato Schlacher: il Motto am Fluss.

D

Hidden in the core of the lively Bermuda Triangle nightlife area, First Floor is one of the most beautiful bars in Vienna. Parts of the interior, such as the superb mahogany ceiling panels, come from the legendary Mounier Bar in Vienna and were carefully integrated into the newer decor by architects Eichinger oder Knechtl. The giant aquarium behind the bar submerges the room in a soft light, and the high quality of the expertly mixed cocktails invite visitors to linger.

Inmitten des belebten Ausgehviertels Bermudadreieck ist das First Floor versteckt, eine der schönsten Wiener Bars. Teile des Interieurs, wie etwa die herrlichen Paneelen aus Mahagoni an der Decke, stammen aus der legendären Wiener Mounier Bar und wurden von den Architekten Eichinger oder Knechtl behutsam in die neuere Ausstattung integriert. Das langgezogene Aquarium hinter dem Tresen taucht den Raum in sanftes Licht und die hohe Qualität der fachgerecht gemixten Cocktailvarianten lädt zum längeren Verweilen ein.

En plein cœur du Bermudadreieck (le triangle des Bermudes), le quartier très prisé des bars et discothèques, se trouve le First Floor, l'un des plus beaux bars de Vienne. Certains éléments de son intérieur comme les superbes lambris en acajou au plafond provenant du Mounier Bar, le légendaire bar viennois, ont été subtilement intégrés au nouvel intérieur par le cabinet d'architectes Eichinger oder Knechtl. Derrière le comptoir, le long aquarium plonge la pièce dans une ambiance tamisée invitant à siroter de délicieux cocktails.

Il First Floor, uno dei bar più belli di Vienna, è nascosto nel quartiere della vita notturna che va sotto il nome di Bermudadreieck (triangolo delle Bermuda). Parti del suo interno, come per esempio i pannelli di legno di mogano del soffitto, risalgono al leggendario Mounier Bar di Vienna e sono state magistralmente inserite nel nuovo arredamento dagli architetti Eichinger oder Knechtl. Il lungo acquario dietro il bancone dona all'ambiente una luce gradevole e gli ottimi cocktail preparati a regola d'arte invitano a momenti di relax.

DESIGN // RESTAURANTS   129

FIRST FLOOR

Seitenstettengasse 5 // 1st district, Innere Stadt
Tel.: +43 (0)1 533 25 23

Mon–Sat 7 pm to 4 am, Sun 7 pm to 3 am
U1, U4 Schwedenplatz

D

RESTAURANT DESIGN BY HERMANN CZECH

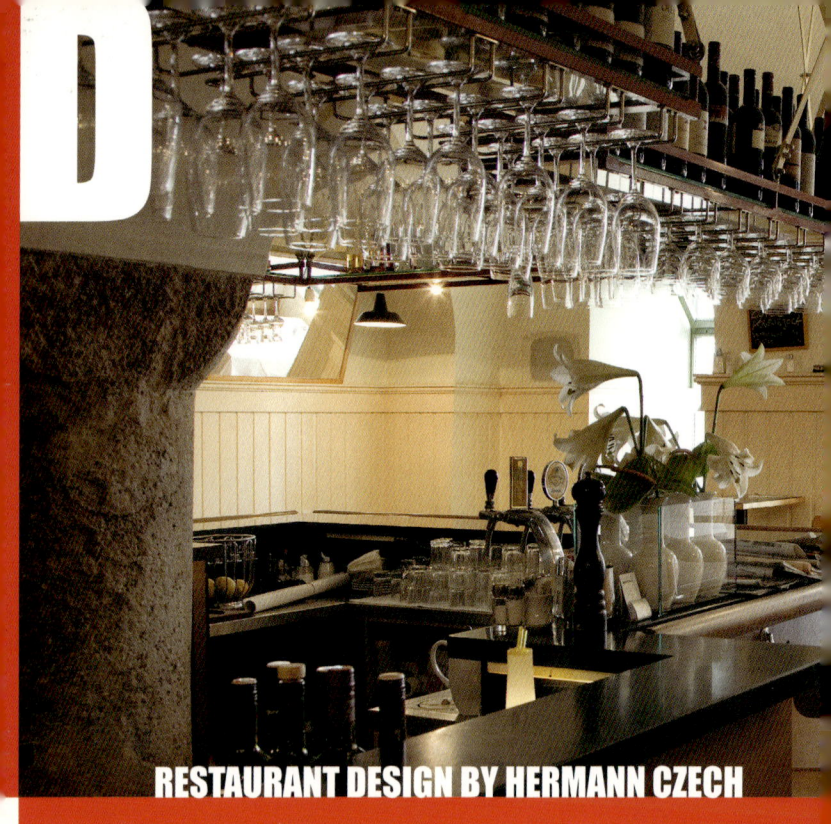

From 1970 to 2000, architect Hermann Czech designed many restaurants and hot spots that are favorites in artistic and creative circles. Despite their differences, the Kleines Café, the Gasthaus Immervoll and the Salzamt have one thing in common: They share a sophisticated design that seems to consist of random elements. From the inconspicuous way the different levels for seating and standing areas are balanced in the Kleines Café to the sliding windows that can be opened with a single finger in the Salzamt—Czech carefully plans every tiny detail.

Von 1970 bis 2000 gestaltete der Architekt Hermann Czech mehrere in der Kunst- und Kreativszene beliebte Lokale. Trotz aller Unterschiedlichkeiten eint das Kleine Café, das Gasthaus Immervoll und das Salzamt die Selbstverständlichkeit, mit der eine ausgeklügelte Komposition aus Zufälligkeiten zu bestehen scheint. Vom unauffällig ausgeglichenen Niveauunterschied zwischen Sitz- und Stehbereich im Kleinen Café bis zu den mit einem Finger bedienbaren Schiebefenstern im Salzamt – Czechs stringente Sorgfalt lässt kein Detail außer Acht.

DESIGN // RESTAURANTS   131

De 1970 à 2000, l'architecte Hermann Czech a conçu plusieurs lieux dédiés à l'art et la création qui rencontrent un franc succès. Bien que différents, le Kleines Café, le Gasthaus Immervoll et le restaurant Salzamt affichent tous trois une composition réussie de détails qui semblent être le fruit du hasard. De la différence de niveau entre l'espace tables et l'espace bar discrètement atténuée du Kleines Café aux fenêtres du Salzamt se coulissant avec un seul doigt, Czech a soigné les moindres détails.

Tra il 1970 e il 2000 l'architetto Hermann Czech ha realizzato diversi locali molto apprezzati da artisti e persone creative. Nonostante la loro diversità, il Kleines Café, la Gasthaus Immervoll e il Salzamt sono accomunati dalla naturalezza di questa sapiente fusione di accidentalità. Dal modo discreto con cui nel Kleines Café si passa dall'elegante zona con tavolini a quella più informale della zona bar, fino alla finestra scorrevole manovrabile con un dito nel Salzamt, l'estrema accuratezza di Czech non trascura alcun dettaglio.

D

KLEINES CAFÉ

Franziskanerplatz 3 // 1st district, Innere Stadt

Mon–Sun 10 am to 2 am
U1, U3 Stephansplatz

DESIGN // RESTAURANTS   133

IMMERVOLL

Weihburggasse 17 //
1st district, Innere Stadt
Tel.: +43 (0)1 513 52 88

Mo–Sun noon to midnight
U1, U3 Stephansplatz

SALZAMT

Ruprechtsplatz 1 //
1st district, Innere Stadt
Tel.: +43 (0)1 533 53 32
www.salzamt-wien.at

Mon–Sun 5 pm to 2 am
U1, U4 Schwedenplatz

D

LOOSBAR

Kärntner Durchgang 10 // 1st district, Innere Stadt
Tel.: +43 (0)1 512 32 83
www.loosbar.at

Sun–Wed noon to 4 am, Thu–Sat noon to 5 am
U1, U3 Stephansplatz

DESIGN // RESTAURANTS

It pays to show up early because this tiny American Bar, designed in 1908 by Adolf Loos, gets crowded in a hurry—it magically attracts travelers and Viennese who love design. The famous architect used materials such as onyx, marble, wood, and brass in the interior; cleverly placed mirrors gives this architectural gem a feeling of space. Yet watch your step when you descend into the basement: The stairs are steep, and visitors need to be careful especially after having enjoyed a drink or two.

Früh kommen lohnt sich, denn in der winzigen, von Adolf Loos 1908 gestalteten American Bar kann es schnell eng werden, ist sie doch ein magischer Anziehungspunkt für designverliebte Wiener wie für Reisende. Der berühmte Architekt verwendete Materialien wie Onyx, Marmor, Holz und Messing für das Interieur, und geschickt gesetzte Spiegel vergrößern das Kleinod der architektonischen Moderne optisch. Beim Gang ins Souterrain ist Vorsicht geboten: Die steile Treppe erfordert einiges Geschick, vor allem nach dem Genuss der Drinks.

Dans ce bar américain exigu créé en 1908 par Adolf Loos, on est vite à l'étroit, il est donc conseillé de venir tôt. Ce bar est très apprécié des Viennois amoureux de design ainsi que des touristes. Le célèbre architecte a utilisé de l'onyx, du marbre, du bois et du laiton pour réaliser l'intérieur. Des miroirs placés astucieusement permettent d'agrandir optiquement ce petit bijou de l'architecture moderne. Prudence en vous rendant au sous-sol, l'escalier est abrupt et difficile à appréhender surtout après avoir dégusté quelques verres.

Merita arrivare presto in questo bar in stile americano realizzato nel 1908 da Adolf Loos, o si rischia di non trovare posto. Il bar infatti è amato tanto da turisti quanto dagli abitanti di Vienna con un debole per il design. Il famoso architetto utilizzò materiali come onice, marmo, legno e ottone, mentre specchi collocati in posizioni strategiche fanno apparire più grande questo gioiello dell'architettura moderna. Attenti ad accedere al seminterrato: la ripida scala può infatti giocare brutti scherzi, specialmente dopo aver apprezzato gli ottimi drink.

DO & CO WORLD

With his restaurants DO & CO Stephansplatz and DO & CO Albertina, as well as his DO & CO Hotel Vienna across from St. Stephen's Cathedral, Attila Dogudan has created a culinary world of the highest caliber whose reputation extends far beyond Austria. Dogudan is the culinary force behind many global mega events ranging from Formula One Grand Prix racing to soccer championships. One of Vienna's coffee houses especially rich in tradition, the k.u.k. Hofzuckerbäcker Demel on the Kohlmarkt was added to Dogudan's DO & CO universe in 2002.

Attila Dogudan hat mit den Restaurants DO & CO am Stephansplatz und DO & CO Albertina und dem DO & CO Hotel gegenüber dem Stephansdom eine eigene Welt geschaffen, die für eine hohe gastronomische, auch international geschätzte Qualität steht. Nicht umsonst betreut Dogudan viele der globalen Megaevents, ob Formel-1-Grand-Prix oder Fußball-EM, gastronomisch. Seit 2002 gehört die k.u.k.-Hofzuckerbäcker Demel am Kohlmarkt, eines der traditionsreichsten Wiener Kaffeehäuser, zu Dogudans DO & CO-Universum.

DESIGN // RESTAURANTS   137

Avec les restaurants DO & CO Stephanplatz et DO & CO Albertina ainsi que le DO & CO Hotel Vienna en face cathédrale S-Étienne, Attila Dogudan est parvenu à créer un univers où triomphent une haute gastronomie et une qualité de renommée internationale. Ce n'est pas pour rien que Dogudan est le chef gastronomique attitré d'événements internationaux comme le Grand prix de formule 1. Depuis 2002, la k.u.k.-Hofzuckerbäcker Demel du Kohlmarkt, une maison de café viennoise traditionnelle, lui appartient aussi.

Con i ristoranti DO & CO Stephansplatz e DO & CO Albertina e l'albergo DO & CO Hotel Vienna, di fronte al Duomo di S. Stefano, Attila Dogudan ha creato un proprio universo che è simbolo di cucina d'alta qualità apprezzata anche a livello internazionale. Non per niente Dogudan è responsabile dell'organizzazione culinaria di molti eventi di scala mondiale, dal Gran Premio ai di Formula 1. Dal 2002 fa parte del suo impero anche la k.u.k.-Hofzuckerbäcker Demel presso Kohlmarkt, una delle caffetterie di più lunga data della città.

DO & CO HOTEL STEPHANSPLATZ

Stephansplatz 12 // 1st district, Innere Stadt
Tel.: +43 (0)1 241 88
www.doco.com

U1, U3 Stephansplatz

DESIGN // RESTAURANTS   139

DO & CO ALBERTINA

Albertinaplatz 1 //
1st district, Innere Stadt
Tel.: +43 (0)1 532 96 69
www.doco.com

Mon–Sun 9 am to midnight
U1, U2, U4 Karlsplatz/Oper,
U1, U3 Stephansplatz

K.U.K. HOFZUCKERBÄCKER DEMEL

Kohlmarkt 14 //
1st district, Innere Stadt
Tel.: +43 (0)1 535 17 17-0
www.demel.at

Mon–Sun 9 am to 7 pm
U1, U3 Stephansplatz

D

NASCHMARKT

A visit to the Naschmarkt is a must to enjoy a variety of traditional Viennese and exotic specialties (tip: search out the tiny Urbanek booth). The Naschmarkt is a perfect place to eat: aside from classics such as the Umar Fisch restaurant and Café Drechsler designed by Sir Terence Conran, Neni is one of the most interesting newcomers to the market with its international fusion cuisine with Israeli/Asian influences. Also highly recommended is Kim kocht, a restaurant where chef Sohyi Kim offers her fine creations.

Der Besuch des Naschmarkts ist ein Muss, schon wegen der vielen typisch wienerischen und exotischen Spezialitäten (Tipp: der winzige Feinkoststand Urbanek). Auch zum Essengehen ist der Markt sehr empfehlenswert: Neben Klassikern wie dem Fischrestaurant Umar und dem von Sir Terence Conran gestalteten Café Drechsler zählt das Neni mit einer israelisch-orientalisch angehauchten internationalen Fusionküche zu den interessantesten Newcomern. Empfehlenswert auch das Kim kocht, wo Szeneköchin Sohyi Kim ihre feinen Kreationen anbietet.

DESIGN // RESTAURANTS   141

Avec ses nombreuses spécialités viennoises et exotiques, le Naschmarkt est incontournable (On vous recommande le petit stand d'épicerie fine Urbanek). Ce marché est aussi parfait pour assouvir les appétits : à côté des classiques comme le restaurant de poisson Umar et le Café Drechsler pensé par Sir Terence Coran, vous trouverez le Neni, un nouveau né de la gastronomie proposant une cuisine fusion internationale aux accents israélo-orientaux, sans oublier le Kim kocht, où Sohyi Kim, la chef vedette propose ses fines créations.

Il Naschmarkt di Vienna è una tappa d'obbligo, anche solo per le leccornie viennesi ed esotiche che vi si possono acquistare (consigliamo la bancarella di specialità gastronomiche Urbanek). Ma qui si può anche mangiare: accanto a classici come il ristorante di pesce Umar e il Café Drechsler, realizzato da Sir Terence Conran, non mancano new entry tra cui spicca il Neni, che offre una cucina internazionale ispirata a tradizioni israeliano-orientali. Eccellente anche il Kim kocht, dove si possono gustare le creazioni dell'affermata cuoca Sohyi Kim.

D

NENI

Naschmarkt, booth 510 // 6th district, Mariahilf
Tel.: +43 (0)1 585 20 20
www.neni.at

Mon–Sat 8 am to midnight
U4 Kettenbrückengasse

DESIGN // RESTAURANTS 143

UMAR FISCH

Naschmarkt, booth 76–79 // 6th district, Mariahilf
Tel.: +43 (0)1 585 21 77 (shop),
+43 (0)1 587 04 56 (restaurant)
www.umarfisch.at

Mon–Fri 8 am to 6 pm, Sat 8 am to 5 pm (shop),
Mon–Sat 11 am to 11 pm (restaurant)
U1, U2, U4 Karlsplatz/Oper

CAFÉ DRECHSLER

Linke Wienzeile 22 // 6th district, Mariahilf
Tel.: +43 (0)1 581 20 44
www.cafedrechsler.at

Mon 8 am to 2 am, Tue–Sat 3 am to 2 am, Sun 3 am to midnight
U4 Kettenbrückengasse

DESIGN // RESTAURANTS 145

KIM KOCHT

Naschmarkt, booth 28 //
6th district, Mariahilf
Tel.: +43 (0)1 319 34 02
www.kimkocht.at

Tue–Sat noon to 6 pm
U1, U2, U4 Karlsplatz/Oper

URBANEK

Naschmarkt, booth 46 //
6th district, Mariahilf
Tel.: +43 (0)1 587 20 80

Mon 9 am to 6.30 pm,
Tue–Thu 9 am to 6.30 pm,
Fri 8 am to 6.30 pm,
Sat 7.30 am to 4 pm

D

Designed by Gregor Eichinger, Song scores points with its minimalistic aesthetics. Unplastered walls, French industrial lamps from the 1920s and custom clothes racks give the store a chic industrial look. Aside from her Song-by-Song collection, owner Myung-Il Song offers selected pieces from AF Vandevorst to Martin Margiela as well as furniture made from recycled wood by Dutch designer Piet Hein Eek and vintage French furniture. Gallery Song Song adjoins the space.

Mit minimalistischer Ästhetik punktet das von Gregor Eichinger gestaltete Song. Unverputzte Wände, französische Industrielampen aus den 1920ern und extra angefertigte Kleiderstangen verleihen einen schicken Industrial-Look. Besitzerin Myung-Il Song präsentiert neben ihrer Song-by-Song-Kollektion ausgewählte Stücke von AF Vandevorst bis Martin Margiela sowie Möbel aus recyceltem Holz des holländischen Designers Piet Hein Eek und französische Vintagemöbel. Angeschlossen ist die Galerie Song Song.

Dessiné par Gregor Eichinger dans un style minimaliste, le Song vaut le détour. Les murs bruts, les lampes industrielles françaises des années 1920 et les portants à vêtements confèrent à cette boutique un cachet industriel unique. La propriétaire, Myung-Il Song, y présente sa propre collection Song-by-Song et de superbes modèles d'AF Vandevorst ou encore Martin Magiela mais aussi des meubles en bois recyclé du designer hollandais Piet Hein Eek et des meubles vintage français. La galerie Song Song est accolée à la boutique.

Con il suo design minimalista, la boutique Song di Gregor Eichinger coglie nel segno. Pareti non intonacate, lampade industriali francesi degli anni '20 e appendiabiti realizzati su misura donano all'ambiente un raffinato look industriale. Accanto alla sua collezione Song-by-Song, la proprietaria Myung-Il Song presenta abiti scelti di stilisti come AF Vandevorst e Martin Margiela, nonché mobili di legno riciclato del designer olandese Piet Hein Eek e pezzi d'arredamento vintage francesi. Al negozio è annessa la galleria Song Song.

DESIGN // SHOPS 147

SONG / SONG SONG

Praterstraße 11–13 // 2nd district, Leopoldstadt
Tel.: +43 (0)1 532 28 58
www.song.at

Mon 1 pm to 7 pm, Tue–Fri 10 am to 7 pm,
Sat 10 am to 6 pm
U1, U4 Schwedenplatz, U1 Nestroyplatz

D

UNGER UND KLEIN

Gölsdorfgasse 2 // 1st district, Innere Stadt
Tel.: +43 (0)1 532 13 23
www.ungerundklein.at

Mon–Fri 3 pm to midnight, Sat 5 pm to midnight
U1, U4 Schwedenplatz

DESIGN // SHOPS

Is Unger und Klein a wine store where you can sit at small tables and enjoy a wine tasting? Or is it a bar with a small menu where you can order wine by the bottle as a side dish? Designed by Eichinger oder Knechtl and located close to Schwedenplatz, it is actually both. A wine shelf curves around the room and conveniently holds bottles of wine, sparkling wine, spirits, and delicacies from Austria, Italy, France, Spain, and overseas. A changing selection of wines can also be ordered over the phone.

Ist es eine Weinhandlung, in der man an kleinen Tischen die edlen Tropfen auch verkosten kann? Oder eine Bar mit Minispeisekarte, in der man den Wein als Beilage gleich flaschenweise ordert? Das von Eichinger oder Knechtl designte Lokal nahe des Schwedenplatzes ist beides. Das geschwungene, den Raum flankierende Regal hält Weine, Schaumweine, Destillate und Delikatessen aus Österreich, Italien, Frankreich, Spanien und Übersee bereit. Ein wechselndes Sortiment an Weinen kann auch telefonisch bestellt werden.

Unger und Klein est-il un caviste chez qui l'on peut aussi déguster les meilleurs crus à une petite table ? Ou est-ce un bar avec une petite carte où l'on peut commander le vin à la bouteille ? Cet endroit au design signé Eichinger oder Knechtl, situé près de la Schwedenplatz, est les deux à la fois. Sur l'étagère courbée qui flanque la pièce, on trouve des vins, des mousseux, des spiritueux et spécialités d'Autriche, d'Italie, de France et d'outre Atlantique. Il est possible de commander une sélection de vins par téléphone.

Unger und Klein è forse un'enoteca con tanto di tavolini per la degustazione dei suoi nobili vini? O piuttosto un bar con un piccolo menù dove i vini d'accompagnamento possono essere ordinati anche a bottiglia? Questo locale progettato da Eichinger oder Knechtl vicino a Schwedenplatzes è un po' entrambe le cose. Il sinuoso scaffale che lo fiancheggia trabocca di vini, spumanti, distillati e leccornie provenienti da Austria, Italia, Francia, Spagna e oltreoceano. L'assortimento di vini è sempre diverso e può essere ordinato anche telefonicamente.

D

Like blooming sculptures, these precious plants—often several in a series—stand on plain steel shelves. Sleek metal light fixtures emphasize the classy staging in this minimalistic shop. A few steps along towards the Naschmarkt, mood's 2,200-sq.-ft. showroom offers distinctive interior design with inter-national brands ranging from Vitra to Tom Dixon.

Blühenden Skulpturen gleich stehen die edlen Gewächse, oft mehrere in Serie, in nüchternen Stahlregalen. Die stilvolle Inszenierung des minimalistisch gestalteten Shops wird durch schlichte Metallleuchten optimal zur Geltung gebracht. Ein paar Schritte weiter Richtung Naschmarkt bietet das mood im 200 m² großen Schauraum individuelles Interior Design internationaler Marken von Vitra bis Tom Dixon.

DESIGN // SHOPS 151

BLUMENKRAFT

Schleifmühlgasse 4 // 4th district, Wieden
Tel.: +43 (0)1 585 77 27
www.blumenkraft.at

Mon–Fri 10 am to 7 pm, Sat 9 am to 2 pm
Tram 1, 62 Paulanergasse,
Bus 59A Schleifmühlgasse

MOOD

Schleifmühlgasse 13 // 4th district, Wieden
Tel.: +43 (0)1 236 31 31
www.moodwien.at

Tue–Fri 10 am to 6 pm, Sat 10 am to 4 pm
Tram 1, 62 Paulanergasse,
Bus 59A Schleifmühlgasse

À côté des sculptures florales se trouvent de sublimes plantes, souvent présentées en séries sur de sobres étagères d'acier. Le cadre stylé de cette boutique au design épuré est mis en valeur par des luminaires sobres en métal. À quelques enjambées, en direction du Naschmarkt, le mood propose, sur une surface de 200 m², du design d'intérieur de grandes marques internationales comme Vitra ou Tom Dixon.

Simili a sculture floreali, le raffinate piante di questo negozio sono disposte, spesso in serie, in modesti scaffali di acciaio. L'incantevole allestimento di questi negozi di fiori dallo stile minimalista è perfettamente valorizzato da semplici lampade di metallo. A pochi passi di distanza verso Naschmarkt si trova il mood, che in una showroom di 200 m² espone pezzi unici di design degli interni di marchi internazionali come Vitra o Tom Dixon.

D

LICHTERLOH

Gumpendorfer Straße 15–17 // 6th district, Mariahilf
Tel.: +43 (0)1 586 05 20
www.lichterloh.com

Mon–Fri 11 am to 6.30 pm, Sat 11 am to 4 pm
Bus 57A Laimgrubengasse

DESIGN // SHOPS

Lichterloh
Der Wohnverstärker

Lichterloh specializes in Austrian and international furniture design of the 20th century with an emphasis on the 1920s to the 1970s. The showrooms display designs by Arne Jacobsen and Ray and Charles Eames, as well as reproductions of timeless design classics and even the famous stacking city hall chairs with perforated backrest designed by Austrian architect Roland Rainer. New to the lineup is "our small gym saloon" with leather benches, stools and pommel horses from the Czech Republic.

Auf österreichisches und internationales Möbeldesign des 20. Jahrhunderts mit Fokus auf die 1920er bis 1970er Jahre hat sich Lichterloh spezialisiert. Entwürfe von Arne Jacobsen und Ray und Charles Eames finden sich in den Schauräumen ebenso wie Reproduktionen zeitloser Designklassiker oder die berühmten stapelbaren Stadthallen-Stühle mit durchlöcherter Lehne des österreichischen Architekten Roland Rainer. Neu im Sortiment ist die Reihe „unser kleiner Turnsalon" mit Lederbänken, Hockern und Seitpferden aus Tschechien.

Lichterloh, spécialisé dans les meubles design autrichiens et internationaux est surtout consacré à la période des années 1920 à 1970. Dans les show-rooms figurent des ébauches d'Arne Jacobsen, de Ray et Charles Eames ainsi que des reproductions de classiques du design ou les célèbres chaises empilables au dossier perforé de l'architecte autrichien Roland Rainer. Nouveauté : la série « notre petit salon de gymnastique » composée de bancs en cuir, de tabourets et chevaux d'arçons provenant de Tchéquie.

Il Lichterloh è specializzato in pregiati pezzi d'arredamenti austriaci e internazionali del XX secolo, in particolare del periodo compreso tra gli anni '20 e '70. Nelle showroom trovano spazio creazioni di Arne Jacobsen e Ray & Charles Eames, accanto a riproduzioni di classici senza tempo e alle famose sedie impilabili da sala congressi con schienale forato disegnate dall'architetto austriaco Roland Rainer. Nuova la serie "il nostro salone della ginnastica", con panche di pelle, sgabelli e cavalline provenienti dalla Repubblica Ceca.

D

PARK

Mondscheingasse 20 // 7th district, Neubau
Tel.: +43 (0)1 526 44 14
www.park.co.at

Mon–Fri 10 am to 7 pm, Sat 10 am to 6 pm
U3 Neubaugasse

DESIGN // SHOPS   155

The key design element in the two story PARK concept store is the color white: from the walls to the ceiling to the clothes hangers everything is white. Along with current women's and menswear collections from designers such as Ann Demeulemeester, Haider Ackermann or Raf Simons, and Austrian labels ranging from Fabrics Interseason to Pelican Avenue, PARK also carries international fashion and art magazines and books.

Bestimmendes Gestaltungselement im zweigeschossigen Conceptstore PARK ist die Farbe Weiß: Von den Wänden über die Decke bis zu den Kleiderbügeln ist hier alles weiß gestrichen. Neben den aktuellen Womenswear- und Menswear-Kollektionen von Designern wie Ann Demeulemeester, Haider Ackermann oder Raf Simons und österreichischen Labels von Fabrics Interseason bis Pelican Avenue führt das PARK auch internationale Mode- und Kunstmagazine sowie Bücher.

L'élément déterminant de la réalisation du concept store PARK est le blanc : des murs aux plafonds en passant par les cintres tout est peint en blanc. PARK propose les collections homme et femme de créateurs tendance comme Ann Demeulemeester, Haider Ackermann ou Raf Simons et des marques autrichiennes comme Fabrics Interseason ou Pelican Avenue ainsi que des revues internationales de mode et d'art ou encore des livres.

Elemento caratterizzante del PARK, un concept store a due piani, è il colore bianco: dalle pareti al soffitto fino alle grucce, qui tutto quanto è dipinto di bianco. Oltre alle ultime collezioni uomo e donna di stilisti come Ann Demeulemeester, Haider Ackermann e Raf Simons e a griffe austriache che vanno da Fabrics Interseason a Pelican Avenue, PARK propone anche riviste internazionali di moda e d'arte e libri.

INNERE STADT

Vienna's first district with Kärntner Strasse, Graben and Kohlmarkt is a mecca for shoppers—a mixture of traditional Viennese stores, exclusive flagship stores of international labels and designers and numerous high street chains. Look out for the famous Viennese cafés.

ART

Location	N°	page
Augarten Contemporary	1	10
KEX Kunsthalle Exnergasse	2	12
BAWAG Contemporary	3	14
das weisse haus	4	16
COCO	5	18
MAK Austrian Museum of Contemporary Arts	6	22
MAK Depot of Contemporary Arts	7	23
Gefechtsturm Arenbergpark		
Seilerstätte Galleries	8	24
Art Contemporary		
Thyssen-Bornemisza	9	29
Albertina	10	33
Eschenbachgasse Galleries	11	35
MuseumsQuartier	12	39
Secession	13	44
Wien Museum Karlsplatz	14	46
Belvedere	15	48
Schleifmühlgasse Galleries	16	52
Westlicht	17	57
Essl Museum	18	58

ARCHITECTURE

page	N°	Location
64	19	Die Bremer Stadtmusikanten
66	20	Wohnbau Spittelau
68	21	Bahnhof Wien Praterstern
70	22	UNIQA Tower, Sofitel Vienna Stephansdom
74	23	WAGNER:WERK Museum Postsparkasse
78	24	Haas-Haus
80	25	Looshaus
82	26	Architekturzentrum Wien
88	27	IP-TWO
88	28	Wiener Stadthalle
89	29	Hauptbücherei Wien
89	30	Skywalk - Skyline
90	31	Haus Ray 1
92	32	Gasometer
96	33	T-Center St. Marx
100	34	Wienerberg City
104	35	Kabelwerk

MAP 157

MUSEUMSQUARTIER/ 7TH DISTRICT/SPITTELBERG

With its museums, art galleries, photo studios and ateliers, the 7th district is the creative hub of the city. Many of Vienna's fashion designers have opened small shops and offer their collections, from innovative streetwear to sophisticated couture.

DESIGN

page	N°	Location
110	36	Hollmann Beletage
112	37	The Ring - Vienna's Casual Luxury Hotel
116	38	Das Triest
120	39	Skopik & Lohn
124	40	Motto
124	41	Motto am Fluss
125	42	Halle Café-Restaurant
125	43	Kunsthallencafe am Karlsplatz
129	44	First Floor
132	45	Kleines Café
133	46	Immervoll
133	47	Salzamt
134	48	Loosbar
138	49	DO & CO Hotel Stephansplatz
139	50	DO & CO Albertina
139	51	K.U.K. Hofzuckerbäcker Demel
140	52	Naschmarkt
146	53	Song / Song Song
148	54	Unger und Klein
150	55	Blumenkraft, Mood
152	56	Lichterloh
154	57	Park

NASCHMARKT/ SCHLEIFMÜHLGASSE

Over the last years, trendy eateries and bars have almost outnumbered the traditional market stalls at Naschmarkt Market, famous for its Viennese and international specialties. Thanks to its vibrant galleries and design shops, nearby Schleifmühlgasse is a hotspot for the creative and artistic community.

KARMELITERMARKT

With a growing number of bars, studios and galleries, the "Grätzel" (Viennese for neighborhood) around the Karmelitermarkt attracts well-to-do citizens, young artists and hipsters alike. Only a few minutes away, the Donaukanal boasts interesting new buildings from internationally renowned architects as well as city beaches, clubs and bars.

BRUNNENMARKT/ YPPENPLATZ

The Brunnenmarkt is Vienna's largest street market. The vibrant and colorful area exudes a multicultural flair. Numerous artists have moved here. Nearby Yppenplatz is a meeting place for the creative scene, with excellent restaurants, cafés, traditional market stalls, and small shops.

Map of Vienna Districts

9. BEZIRK ALSERGRUND

16. BEZIRK OTTAKRING

8. BEZIRK JOSEFSTADT

7. BEZIRK NEUBAU

6. BEZIRK MARIAHILF

MICHELBEUERN AKH

SCHOTTENTOR

RATHAUSPARK

VOLKSGARTEN

VOLKSTHEATER

WESTBAHNHOF

KETTENBRÜCKENGASSE

Streets

- WÄHRINGERSTR.
- ALSER STR.
- ALSERSTR.
- HERNALSER GÜRTEL
- JOSEFSTADTER STR.
- UNIVERSITÄTSSTR.
- LANDESGERICHTSSTR.
- RATHAUS
- THALIASTR.
- LERCHENFELDERSTR.
- THALIASTR.
- OPPSTR.
- NEUSTIFTGASSE
- BURGG.
- BURGGASSE-STADTHALLE
- KANDLG.
- NEUBAUG.
- SCHOTTENFELDG.
- KAISERSTR.
- WESTBAHNSTR.
- NEUBAUGÜRTEL
- MARIAHILFER STR.
- NEUBAUGASSE
- ZIEGLERGASSE
- MUSEUMSPLATZ
- HELDENPLATZ

Markers

- 18, 2
- 27
- 26, 42, 12, 1
- 28
- 17
- 29
- 57
- 56
- 52
- 34, 35
- 40
- 3

MAP 159

2. BEZIRK LEOPOLDSTADT

1. BEZIRK INNERE STADT

WIEN

BURGGARTEN

KARLSPLATZ

RESSELPARK

STADTPARK

3. BEZIRK LANDSTRASSE

BELVEDERE GARTEN

EMERGENCY

Fire   Tel.: 122
Police   Tel.: 133
Ambulance   Tel.: 144
European emergency number 112

ARRIVAL

BY PLANE
Vienna International Airport (VIE) 10 miles / 16 km southeast of the city center. National and international flights. Take the City Airport Train (CAT) to the City Air Terminal at Wien Mitte (16 min.) or the express train line (S-Bahn) S7 to Wien Mitte and Wien Nord railway stations (25 min.). Take the Vienna Airport Line buses to Schwedenplatz/Morzinplatz (20 min.), to Wien Meidling (30 min.) and Wien Westbahnhof (45 min.) railway stations.

Flight information:
Tel.: +43 (0)1 700 72 22 33
www.viennaairport.com

BY TRAIN
WIEN WESTBAHNHOF
Direct connection to numerous S-Bahn lines, subway lines U3 and U6 and trams

WIEN MEIDLING
Throughout the construction works of the Central Station, Wien Meidling railway station partly replaces Südbahnhof. Direct connection to numerous S-Bahn lines, U6 subway line (station Philadelphiabrücke), trams, buses and the Wiener Lokalbahn (Vienna Local Rail).

SÜDBAHNHOF (OSTBAHN)
The eastbound rail services of Südbahnhof remain in operation throughout the construction works of the Central Station. Direct connection to numerous S-Bahn lines, trams and buses.

www.oebb.at – Official Website of the Austrian Federal Railways (ÖBB),
Tel.: +43 (0)5 17 17

TOURIST INFORMATION

WienTourismus (Vienna Tourist Board)
Obere Augartenstraße 40
1020 Vienna
Tel.: +43 (0)1 245 55
Fax: +43 (0)1 245 55-666

info@wien.info (to order information material, ticket and hotel reservations, vacation packages)

Vienna Tourist Information is located at Albertinaplatz (1st district), open daily from 9 am to 7 pm for information, hotel bookings, Vienna Card, brochures, souvenirs, postcards, stamps. Sale of tickets for opera, concerts, theater and cultural events, sightseeing, day trips as well as train tickets. Another information point is located at Vienna International Airport (Arrival Hall), open daily from 6 am to 11 pm.

www.wien.info –
Vienna Tourist Board website
www.wien.at – Official website of Vienna
www.wien.gv.at/stadtplan/en –
Vienna city map

ACCOMMODATION

hotels.wien.info – Hotel booking service of the Vienna Tourist Board
www.tiscover.com/wien – Hotels, apartments, bed & breakfast, etc.

TICKETS

www.oeticket.com – Wide range of tickets for concerts, cabaret, theater and other events in Vienna

The Vienna Card – Unlimited free travel by underground, bus and tram for 72 hours as well as more than 210 discounts at museums and sights, theaters and concerts, in shops, cafés and restaurants. Available online at **www.wienkarte.at/card-order/order.php** as well as in the tourist info points at Albertinaplatz and at the airport, numerous hotels, at sales and information points of the Vienna Transport Authority or by credit card via Tel.: +43 (0)1 798 44 00-148. A ticket for 72 hours costs 18.50 €.

GETTING AROUND

PUBLIC TRANSPORTATION
www.wienerlinien.at –
Wiener Linien (Vienna Transport Authority), Tel.: +43 (0)1 7909-100

TAXI
Tel.: +43 (0)1 601 60, +43 (0)1 401 00, +43 (0)1 313 00

BICYCLE RENTALS
www.citybikewien.at – Tel.: +43 (0)810 500 50-0. Registration online or directly at the Citybike Terminal with a credit card. Rent: 1st hour free, further rent see website. Payment is by credit card.
www.viennaexplorer.com – Tel.: +43 (0)1 890 96 82. Rent is 4 €/hour or 17 €/day.

www.pedalpower.at –
Tel.: +43 (0)1 729 72 34. With bicycle delivery to hotels. Rent is 5 €/hour or 27 €/day. Offers guided city bike tours.

CAR RENTAL
Beside the international rental car companies, there are some Vienna based like:
www.easymotion.at,
www.megadrive.at
www.unioncar.at

CITY TOURS

BUSES AND TRAMWAYS
Taking the bus or tram is the cheapest way of touring the city. A tramway ride on line 1 takes you from the State Opera House, following the Ringstraße and across the Donaukanal, to the Vienna Prater. The Vienna Ring Tram takes you around the Ringstraße with famous sights as the State Opera House, the Imperial Palace, the Parliament, and the Vienna City Hall.

SIGHTSEEING BUSES
www.viennasightseeing.at/EHOPON.htm – Vienna Sightseeing Tours,
Tel.: +43 (0)1 712 46 83-0
www.cityrama.at – Cityrama Sightseeing Tours, Tel.: +43 (0)1 504 75 00
www.redbuscitytours.at – Red Bus City Tours, Tel.: +43 (0)1 512 40 30

BOAT TOURS
www.ddsg-blue-danube.at – DDSG Blue Danube, Tel.: +43 (0)1 588 80
www.twincityliner.com – Twin City Liner, on the Danube to Bratislava,
Tel.: +43 (0)1 588 80

GUIDED TOURS
www.wienguide.at – Walks in Vienna, Tel.: +43 (0)1 774 89 01 – Wide variety of themed tours from the elegant palaces of the Habsburg Empire to the movie locations of The Third Man
www.viennaguideservice.at – Vienna Guide Service, Tel.: +43 (0)1 786 24 00 – Walks around the city with a focus on history, culture and politics
www.wienerwelten.at – Wiener Welten – Worlds of Vienna, Tel.: +43 (0)1 979 83 93 – Walking tours focusing on architecture and history
www.verliebtinwien.at – Vienna with Love, Tel.: +43 (0)1 889 28 06 – Tours on historical themes

ART AND ARCHITECTURAL GUIDES TOURS
www.azw.at/page.php?node_id=100 – Architecture tours and excursions organized by the Architekturzentrum Wien
www.ticket-w.at – Guided sightseeing tours with architects
www.oegfa.at – The Austrian Society for Architecture (ÖGFA) offers guided visits to contemporary buildings and building sites.

ART & CULTURE

www.wien.gv.at/ma53/museen – Alphabetical index of museums and art collections in Vienna
www.kulturleben.at/lang/en/tipps/Museums.xml – Short description of federal museums in Vienna
www.artmagazine.cc – Information about exhibitions and gallery openings in Vienna
blog.esel.at/termine – Art event calendar
www.wienarchitektur.at – Calendar of architecture events in Vienna
www.nextroom.at/event – Calendar of architecture events
www.koer.or.at/en/ – Information about permanent and temporary artistic projects in the public space in Vienna
www.pureaustriandesign.com – Online platform for Austrian design with event calendar
www.austrianfashion.net – Platform of Austrian fashion creatives with event calendar
vienna.unlike.net – City guide for the mobile generation
www.inoperable.at/urbanmap.pdf – Downloadable city guide for all things urban with map of shops, restaurants, galleries, and legal graffiti spots
Art magazine iArtGuide. App download for iPhone at http://itunes.apple.com/at/app/iartguide/id339001893?mt=8

GOING OUT

www.falter.at/wwei
www.play.fm/events
www.volume.at
www.technoboard.at
www.party.at

EVENTS

www.falter.at – Online city magazine
www.stadtbekannt.at – Well-arranged event calendar
www.nightline.cc – Event calendar
termine.orf.at/fm4 – Event calendar of Austrian's biggest alternative music radio station FM4

JANUARY TO MARCH

www.nextroom.at/turn-on – The Turn On architecture festival takes place every two years in March
www.soundframe.at – sound:frame is an audio/visual festival with exhibitions, live events, workshops, screenings and discussion, every year in March/April companied by various additional cultural events.
www.viennaale.de – In early February; attended by many international movie stars; showing top movies

SERVICE

APRIL TO JUNE
www.modepalast.com – Trade fair for fashion, jewelry and accessories, in April every year

www.viennafair.at – International contemporary art fair focused on CEE, takes place beginning of May every year

www.architekturtage.at – Architekturtage, with open house days in architects' offices, specialist guided tours, excursions in Vienna, visits to construction sites, lectures, discussions, films, festivals, and art events, taking place in May

JULY TO SEPTEMBER
www.mqviennafashionweek.com – MQ Vienna Fashion Week with fashion shows, side events and exhibitions, takes place in September

www.viennabiennale.com – Viennabiennale is a contemporary fine arts festival; taking place from September to November every two years

OCTOBER TO DECEMBER
www.viennadesignweek.at – During the design festival in the beginning of October the whole city becomes a platform and showplace of design

www.blickfang.com/wien – Blickfang, international design fair for furniture, fashion and jewelry, takes place in October

langenacht.orf.at – Long night of museums, takes place in October

www.viennale.at – Austria's most important international film festival, takes place every October in beautiful cinemas in Vienna's historic centre

viennaartweek.at – Vienna Art Week with exhibition openings, guided tours, panel discussions, and studio visits, art in the public realm and performances, in November

CREDITS   165

Cover photo (Albertina) by Roland F. Bauer

ART

p 10 (Augarten Contemporary) photos left courtesy of Belvedere/APA-OTS/Ludwig Schedl, middle courtesy of Belvedere, Wien, right; p 11 exhibition "tanzimat", 2010, photo by Lisa Rastl

p 12, 13 (KEX Kunsthalle Exnergasse) exhibition "No more bad girls?", 2010, curated by Kathrin Becker and Claudia Marion Stemberger, photos by Lizzy Courage (further mentioned as lc) and Martin Nicholas Kunz (further mentioned as mnk)

p 14, 15 (BAWAG Contemporary) photos courtesy of BAWAG Contemporary, p 14 photos by Kurt Kuball, p 15 photo by Hertha Hurnaus, architecture by propeller z, hosted by Christian and Franziska Hausmaninger

p 16 (das weisse haus) artwork by Markus Hofer; p 17 left Roland Rauschmeier, middle Timothy Segers, photos by lc/mnk

p 18, 19 (COCO) artwork and photos courtesy of COCO

p 20, 21 (MAK), p 22 left, right photos by Gerald Zugmann/MAK; p 22 middle permanent facade installation "MAKlite" by James Turrell, photo by Margherita Spiluttini/MAK; p 23 (MAK Depot) left "CAT Open 2004 BASE", photo by Karl Michalski/MAK, middle artwork "Vergessen" by Brigitte Kowanz, photos middle, right by MAK/Georg Mayer

p 24, 25 (Galleries Seilerstätte) installation "Der verlorene und wiedergefundene Himmel" by Nick Oberthaler; p 26 middle installation "Habitación retorcida" by Tillman Kaiser, both Layr Wuestenhagen, 2009; p 26 (Nächst St. Stephan) right, p 27, left, 1st, 2nd, 3rd photo mnk/lc; p 27 middle artwork "Po(l)etical", 2009 by Kader Attia, right "Artists of the Gallery, a Special Selection", 2009, photos by Angelika Krinzinger, courtesy of Galerie Krinzinger, Wien

p 28 (Thyssen-Bornemisza Art Contemporary), left Polyester and stainless steel tubes "Staircase-V", 2008 by Do Ho Suh, dimension site specific, Thyssen-Bornemisza Art Contemporary, installation view "A Question of Evidence", Thyssen-Bornemisza Art Contemporary, 2008, photo by Ulrich Dertschei / T-B A21, p 28 middle 18 video projections on monitors, 9 soundtracks (embedded), varying durations "The KD Vyas Correspondence Vol.1", 2006 by Raqs Media Collective, dimension site specific, Thyssen-Bornemisza Art Contemporary, installation view "Shooting Back", Thyssen-Bornemisza Art Contemporary, 2007, photo by Ulrich Dertschei / T-B A21, p 28 right Audio-video installation "Related Legs (Yokohama Dandelions)", 2001 by Pipilotti Rist, dimension site specific, Thyssen-Bornemisza Art Contemporary, installation view "Other than Yourself. An Investigation between Inner and Outer Space", Thyssen-Bornemisza Art Contemporary, 2008, photo by Michael Strasser / T-B A21; p 29 audio and light installation "Ghost", 2010 by Ayşe Erkmen, courtesy of the artist and Galerie Barbara Weiss, Berlin, commissioned by Thyssen-Bornemisza Art Contemporary and Vehbi Koç Foundation, installation view "Tactics of Invisibility", Thyssen-Bornemisza Art Contemporary, 2010, photo by Michael Strasser / T-BA21

p 32 (Albertina) left New Hall for Contemporary Art, photo by Rupert Steiner, right Harriet Hartmann Court, courtesy of Albertina, Wien;

p 33 photo by Roland F. Bauer

p 34, 35 (Eschenbachgasse Galleries) art "The Female Gaze at the Male or Unmale Man", 2009 by Elke Krystufek, Galerie Meyer Kainer, photo courtesy of Galerie Meyer Kainer; p 36 (Krobath) left, art exhibition Julian Opie, 2008, left middle exhibition Seijla Kameric, 2010, (Martin Janda) middle, right photos courtesy of Martin Janda; p 36 photos by Wolfgang Woessner; p 37 (Meyer Kainer) left exhibition gelatin, Palais Keiner Meyer, 2009, left middle exhibition "Precarious Form / Prekäre Skulpturen", curated by Veit Loers, 2009, photos courtesy of Meyer Kainer, middle right (Steinek) art by Robert Barry, 2006, photo by Peter Achhorner, right art "Mr Big" by Ilse Haider, photo by Carol Tachdjian

p 38, 39 (MuseumsQuartier Kunsthalle Wien) exhibition "Skulptur. Prekärer Realismus zwischen Melancholie und Komik", photo by Christian Wachter; p 50 left photo facade courtesy of

MUMOK, middle exhibition "Konstellationen – Sammeln für ein neues Jahrhundert", 2010, photo courtesy of MUMOK, right photo facade by mnk; p 41 left exterior, middle right installation hall, right exhibition "True Romance. Allegorien der Liebe von der Renaissance bis heute", photos by Rüdiger Ettl, courtesy of Kunsthalle Wien; p 42 (Leopold Museum) exterior photos by mnk, poster painting by Egon Schiele; p 43 (Tanzquartier Wien) left, right photos by Kristina Feuchter, middle right "Lucinda Childs", photo by Sally Cohn, all courtesy of Tanzquartier Wien
p 44 (Secession) photo by mnk; p 45 photos left by lc, middle, right by Roland F. Bauer
p 46 (Künstlerhaus – k/haus) left art by Marlene Haring, Passagegalerie, 2009, photo by Nadine Wille, left middle facade photo courtesy of Künstlerhaus k/haus, middle installation by Rudi Molacek, 2007, photo by Pez Hejduk, right art "Dressed to kill", 2006 by Ona B., photo by Marianne Greber; p 47 (Wien Museum Karlsplatz) atrium photo by mnk, middle painting "Dame in Gelb"1899, by Max Kurzweil, courtesy of Wien Museum, right WM-Foyer, photo by Hertha Hurnaus, courtesy of Wien Museum
p 48/49 (Oberes Belvedere) photo by Roland F. Bauer; p 50, 51 (Unteres Belvedere) photos by mnk
p 52, 53 (Schleifmühlgasse Galleries), exhibition "G.R.A.M., café paparazzi", 2009, courtesy of Christine König, Vienna; p 54 (Christine König) left, facade with drawings of Dan Perjovschi, 2007, courtesy of Christine König, Vienna, left middle orange neon installation on ceiling "Mehr Licht", 2008 by Adel Abdessemed, courtesy of Ellipse Foundation, Lisboa and Christine König, Vienna, (Engholm) middle installation "DRAGO PERSIC", 2010, courtesy of Kerstin Engholm, photo by Karl Kühn, middle right installation "My_Never_Ending_Burial_Plot", 2010 by Constanze Ruhm, courtesy of Kerstin Engholm, photo by Karl Kühn, right installation by Dirk Skreber and Claus Föttinger, 2010, courtesy of Kerstin Engholm, photo by Claus Föttinger; p 55 (Gabriele Senn) left painting by Marcel Hüppauff, 2007, left middle art "Meteorites Powder for the Face: Beauty (III)", 2007 and "Rocks (III)", 2007 by Josephine Pryde, middle "Golders Green", 2008 and "Noodeldoodelbutterfly", 2008 by Sarah Staton, photos by Rainer Iglar, courtesy of Gabriele Senn, Vienna, middle right (Georg Kargl Fine Arts) art by Markus Schinwald, 2009, right exhibition "Personal Structures: Time – Space – Existence", 2010, courtesy of Georg Kargl Fine Arts, Vienna
p 56 (WestLicht) photo by mnk; p 57 left, left middle, right photos by lc, middle photo by mnk
p 58 (Essl Museum) photo by Georg Riha; p 59 left, right photos by C. Richters, courtesy of Bilderdepot Essl Museum, Klosterneuburg/Wien

ARCHITECTURE

p 64, 65 (Die Bremer Stadtmusikanten) architecture and photos by ARTEC Architekten, Vienna
p 66, 67 (Wohnbau Spittelau) architecture by Zaha Hadid, photos courtesy of WienTourismus, Karl Thomas
p 68, 69 (Bahnhof Wien Praterstern) architecture by Albert Wimmers, public design courtyard by Boris Podrecca, photos by ÖBB, Robert Deopito
p 70, 71 (UNIQA Tower) architecture by Heinz Neumann, photo by mnk; p 72 left, right and p 73 left photos by mnk, left middle by lc; p 73 (Sofitel Vienna Stephansdom) architecture by Jean Nouvel, photos middle, right by mnk
p 74–77 (WAGNER:WERK Museum Postsparkasse) architecture by Otto Wagner; p 74, 75 photo by Manfred Kostal/Pixelstorm; p 76 left photo by Achim Bednorz, middle photo by Luzia Ellert, right and p 77 photo by Achim Bednorz, all courtesy by WAGNER:WERK Museum
p 78, 79 (Haas-Haus) architecture by Hans Hollein, photos p 78 left by Peter Rigaud, right by Gerhard Weinkirn, p 79 by Nanja Antonczyk, all courtesy of Wien Tourismus
p 80, 81 (Looshaus) architecture by Adolf Loos, photos by mnk
p 82, 83 (Architekturzentrum Wien) architecture by Lacaton & Vassal, p 82 and p 83 left photos by Rupert Steiner, p 83 middle, right exhibition "x projekte der arbeitsgruppe 4", 2010, photo by Pez Hejduk
p 86, 87 (Gürtel) IP-TWO by architects BKK-3, photo by Rupert Christanell; p 88 left (IP-TWO)

CREDITS

photo by Hertha Hurnaus, right (Stadthalle, Halle F), architecture by Dietrich/Untertrifaller, photos by Rupert Christanell; p 89 left (Hauptbücherei Wien) architecture by Ernst Mayr, photo by Manfred Seidl, middle right and right (Skywalk + Skyline) architecture by Tillner & Willinger, RAHM, Bulant & Wailzer, photos middle right by Rupert Christanel, right courtesy of www.porr.at

p 90, 91 (House Ray1) architecture by Delugan Meissl Associated Architects, photos p 90 by Peter Rigaud, Shotview Photographers; p 91 by Hertha Hurnaus

p 92–95 (Gasometer) p 92, 93 architecture "Gasometer C" by Wehdorn Architekten, p 94 "Gasometer C" by Wehdorn Architekten, "Gasometer B" by Coop Himmelb(l)au, p 95 left middle "Gaso-meter C" by Wehdorn Architekten, right "Gasometer B" by Coop Himmelb(l)au, all photos by Gasometer City/APA-OTS/Thomas Preiss

p 96–99 (T Center St. Marx) architecture by Domenig, Eisenköck, Peyker, photos p 96, 97, p 99 middle by mnk, p 98, 99 left, right by lc,

p 100–103 (Wienerberg City) p 100, 101 architecture "Tower A + C" by Coop Himmelb(l)au, "Familienhilfe Bauteile C2 + D2" by atelier4architects, "Delugan Meissl Tower" and „City Lofts Wienerberg" by Delugan Meissl Associated Architects, "Monte Verde" by Albert Wimmer, Semir Zubcevic, "Vienna Twin Towers" by Massimiliano Fuksas, Business Apartments by Cuno Brullmann; p 102 left Architecture "Tower C" by Coop Himmelb(l)au, "Business Apartments" by Cuno Brullmann, "City Lofts Wienerberg" by Delugan Meissl Associated Architects, middle "Familienhilfe Bauteile C2 + D2" by atelier4architects, right "solar waves" architecture by DI Gert M.Mayr-Keber, p 103 (hanging gardens) architecture by Günter Lautner, Nicolaj Kirisits, all photos by mnk

p 104, 105 (Kabelwerk) architecture p 104, 105 left "H Griessergarten" by DI Martin Wurnig in collaboration with Branimir Kljajic, K building sit JG by Hermann & Valentiny und Partner, p 105 left middle "D.1 Terrassenhaus" by Mascha & Seethaler Architekten, right "Y Frauenwohnprojekt" [ro*sa] KalYpso by Werkstatt Wien/Markus Spiegelfeld

DESIGN

p 110 (Hollmann Beletage) photos left, middle by Roland F. Bauer, right and p 111 courtesy by rh. Hotelbetrieb GmbH

p 112–115 (The Ring – Vienna's Casual Luxury Hotel), photos by mnk, p 115 right by lc

p 116–119 (Das Triest) photos by mnk

p 120, 121 (Skopik & Lohn) photos by mnk

p 122–125 (Motto World), p 122, 123 (Kunsthallencafé am Karlsplatz) photo by mnk; p 124 left (Motto) courtesy of Motto Group, middle (Motto) and right (Motto am Fluss) photo by Marianne Greber; p 125 (Halle Café-Restaurant) photo by mnk, left middle, (Kunsthallencafé am Karlsplatz) middle photo by mnk, middle right, right photo by lc

p 128 (First Floor), p 129 left, right photos by lc, middle photo by mnk

p 130–133 (Hermann Czech), p 130, 131 (Immervoll) photo by mnk; p 132 (Kleines Café) left, middle photos by mnk, right photo by lc; p 133 (Immervoll) left, middle photos by lc, middle left photo by mnk, (Salzamt) middle right, right photo by mnk

p 134 (Loosbar) left, right, p 135 photos by mnk, p 134 middle photo by lc

p 136–139 (DO & CO World) p 136, 137 (DO & CO Albertina), p 138 (DO & CO Hotel am Stephansplatz), p 139 left, left middle (DO & CO Albertina), right, right middle (k.u.k. Hofzuckerbäcker Demel) photos by Roland F. Bauer

p 140–145 (Naschmarkt) p 140, 141 (Neni) art by Eva Beresin, photo by lc; p 142 (Neni) art by Eva Beresin; p 143 (Umar Fisch) photos by mnk; p 144 (Café Drechsler), left, left middle, middle right photos by mnk; right photo by lc; p 145 (Kim kocht) left, left middle photos by lc, (Urbanek) middle right photo by mnk, right photo by lc

p 146, 147 (Song / Song Song) photos courtesy of Song

p 148 (Unger und Klein) left, left middle, middle photos by lc, right, p 149 photos by mnk

p 150 (Blumenkraft) photos by mnk; p 151 (Mood) courtesy of Mood

p 152, 153 (Lichterloh) photos courtesy of lichterloh_design, kunst und antiquitäten

p 154, 155 (PARK) photos courtesy of PARK

© 2010 Idea & concept by Martin Nicholas Kunz, Lizzy Courage Berlin
Selected, edited and produced by Isabella Klausnitzer, Isatrends, Wien
Texts by Isabella Klausnitzer, Claudia Hubmann
Editorial coordination and production management: Claudia Hubmann, Martin Nicholas Kunz
Copy editing: Arndt Jasper, Sabine Scholz
Art direction: Lizzy Courage Berlin
Imaging and pre-press: printworks Druckdienstleistungen GmbH, mace.Stuttgart
Translations: Übersetzungsbüro RR Communications Romina Russo, Heather Bock (English),
Élodie Gallois (French), Federica Benetti (Italian)
Special thanks to The Ring - Vienna's Casual Luxury Hotel and Das Triest

© 2010 teNeues Verlag GmbH + Co. KG, Kempen

teNeues Verlag GmbH + Co. KG
Am Selder 37, 47906 Kempen // Germany
Phone: +49 (0)2152 916-0, Fax: +49 (0)2152 916-111
e-mail: books@teneues.de

Press department // Andrea Rehn
Phone: +49 (0)2152 916-202, e-mail: arehn@teneues.de

teNeues Publishing Company
7 West 18th Street, New York, NY 10011 // USA
Phone: +1 (0)212 627 9090, Fax: +1 (0)212 627 9511

teNeues Publishing UK Ltd.
21 Marlowe Court, Lymer Avenue, London SE19 1LP // Great Britain
Phone: +44 (0)20 8670 7522, Fax: +44 (0)20 8670 7523

teNeues France S.A.R.L.
39, rue des Billets, 18250 Henrichemont // France
Phone: +33 (0)2 48 26 93 48, Fax: +33 (0)1 70 72 34 82

www.teneues.com

Picture and text rights reserved for all countries.
No part of this publication may be reproduced in any manner whatsoever.
All rights reserved.

While we strive for utmost precision in every detail, we cannot be held responsible
for any inaccuracies, neither for any subsequent loss or damage arising.
Bibliographic information published by the Deutsche Nationalbibliothek.
The Deutsche Nationalbibliothek lists this publication in the Deutsche Nationalbibliografie;
detailed bibliographic data are available in the Internet at http://dnb.d-nb.de.

Printed in the Czech Republic
ISBN: 978-3-8327-9434-7

MIX
Aus verantwortungs-
vollen Quellen
FSC® C005833

PUBLISHED IN THE SAME SERIES

ISBN 978-3-8327-9433-0

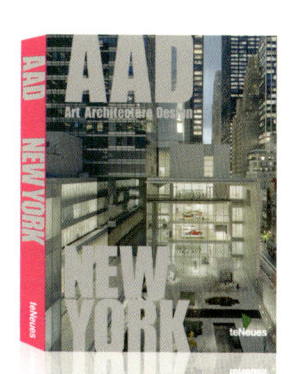

ISBN 978-3-8327-9435-4

UPCOMING TITLES
BARCELONA, LONDON + PARIS